MAR 07 02 -C $\mathcal{B}c$

Dedicated to the editors,
devoted and talented, who served
on the staff of the American Baptist
Board of Education and Publication
during the years 1961-1967.

Living in the Presence of God

Glenn H. Asquith

JUDSON PRESS, Valley Forge

LIVING IN THE PRESENCE OF GOD

International Standard Book No. 0-8170-0559-5
Library of Congress Catalog Card No. 71-183649

Printed in the U.S.A.

Preface

"Will you take the devotions, please?"

This urgent request of a committee chairman or other person responsible for getting a "service" together is all too indicative of the small degree of importance placed on that part of a meeting consisting of a Scripture reading, a prayer, a hymn, and, if time allows, a short meditation. Speaking of time, the one who is persuaded to "take the devotions" usually is warned to "make it brief."

Recognizing this casual treatment of what we call the devotional, we should not be surprised when we turn to a dictionary and find a definition somewhat like this: The common use of the word "devotion" is profound dedication, but the theological usage is religious observance.

As we think about it, we know that a quick and superficial religious observance of the devotional is robbing us and our world of the tremendous power that lies in the depths of communion with God. In our search for the Eternal we should experience power like the swelling tide of an ocean rather than the feeble strength of a noisy, babbling brook.

The chapters of this book are presented as one effort toward an exploration of the mighty possibilities of a genuine devotional life.

1

God's Nearness Discovered

Starting Points: Psalm 63:1-8; Acts 10:1-8, 30-33.

"This is how your dollar is spent."

What a familar statement to us who must pay taxes and who are persuaded to give money to various causes! Budget committees and public relations people eagerly try to show us how efficiently our dollars are put to work at worthwhile and essential projects in the world. Many times we are presented with a chart showing a silver dollar divided into "pie slices." The dollar which goes for taxes is cut up into slices for military expenditures, educational services, health and welfare, administration, internal security, and like expenses of today's life. The dollar given to a church or denomination is marked off for overhead, mission work, schools and colleges, pension board, world relief, and other necessary funding.

Suppose that we could make up our own chart and divide one day into pie slices illustrating the use of each minute, each hour. No doubt there would be wedges for work, leisure-time activities, sleep, television viewing, reading, conversation, and eating. But would there be a slice of any size for devotional time? If so, how large would that slice be in the day of any one of us? If we would look at the completed chart, we probably would be troubled to think of how unimportant we make our search for God. After meditating on the problem, we might come up with the compelling answer that the devotional life of a person cannot be put in a neat pie slice alongside daily occupations. One's devotional life is more than eating, drinking, working, and playing; it is in a class all by itself. The devotional life must be indicated on the chart of the day as the outer rim that touches and holds together all the rest.

Yet, in all honesty, we know that we fail frequently in this ideal of a devotional life that, by communion with the Creator, holds all of life together in a meaningful whole. Often we would have to confess that the time allotted for a devotional life is in the pie slice called "church attendance."

How, then, can we be possessed of a vibrant devotional life by which the nearness of God is in our consciousness minute by minute, hour by hour, day by day, year by year? After all, what is this that we term a "devotional life"? And how shall we discover the way to it? An excellent start on our quest is to follow the footprints of some who have found their way into the very presence of the Eternal.

One such person is the writer of Psalm 63, David, in the opinion of some scholars. Let us think of him on his amazing rise from shepherd boy to king of all Israel.

A "dry and weary land"

In Psalm 63 David confesses that he finds himself fainting for God as he would physically in a "dry and weary land." No doubt this illustration comes from the waterless, desert spots through which David wandered, but the real meaning of his condition is beyond the physical and lies in terms of inner aridity and unrest. David felt as we and as all men, women, and young people feel at times when depression and despair descend. Even in affluence and worldly security, these periods of inner anguish cannot be avoided. At these times the devotional life becomes shade from heat and water to quench thirst. Let us observe how David brought to bear the resources that he found only in God.

David was wise enough to recognize and admit his need for something outside himself and greater than himself. He was out in the world constantly, and more often than not he found the world a place of spiritual hunger and thirst. A reading of any newspaper for any day of any year will illustrate that our world is as the world that David knew. We may read of many fighting a desperate battle just for the bare necessities of life (including equality and dignity), of those who have managed to lay hold of the necessities and are now struggling for a few luxuries to make life richer, and of those who have both necessities and some luxuries and are busy trying to secure even more despite the needs of others. Thefts, wars, murders, and alienation from God occur as a result of these struggles for things. As with David in his day, the conditions in our time speak of the dire need for a knowledge of and companionship with God. The recognition of our compelling need for communion with the Eternal becomes our first step toward the devotional life.

"Steadfast love"

Turning from the clamor, turmoil, selfishness, and suffering of the world, David looked away for a time and came to a realization of God's infinite worth. David found in God steadfast love which, in comparison, made ambitions and possessions like dust. Even the lightest favor of God seemed to bulk larger than the kingship of a great nation. In our time when we have things that David could not imagine and in such profusion that David on his throne would seem a pauper, a moment of valuing must come. Can we find something in God that means more to us than knowledge and things? No devotional life worthy of the name is possible until God is seen as the choicest and best of all that may be experienced by heart, mind, and body. When this glad recognition comes, the seeker will begin to enter into serenity and peace. He will fall back on the steadfast love of God and be comforted and empowered.

Thoughts at night

At this point David discovered something more that we need to find. The devotional life is not like a jewel that, once obtained, may be put in a safe place for future enjoyment; rather it is like a seed planted in a garden that demands unremitting cultivation. There is too much in God and too much available from God to be known and grasped with instant finality. Therefore, David made a practice of meditating about God. He found that uninterrupted times for meditation were the moments between the time he went to bed and the time he fell asleep. He spent these minutes thinking about the goodness and love of God.

David's night habit may be contrasted in our day with the frenzied efforts so many make to avoid insomnia. A pill manufacturer advises us to wait for sleep fifteen minutes, after which we are justified in taking a sleeping sedative! Recently a famous entertainer confessed that he could never go to sleep without the aid of alcohol or drugs. Contrasted with this fear of sleeplessness is the attitude of a person like David earnestly trying to cultivate a rich devotional life; he will be grateful for these highly cherished minutes of wakefulness since they afford him an opportunity for reviewing the glory, mercy, love, forgiveness, and protection of God.

In church

Following on in the experience of David in his devotional life, we find that he went to the sanctuary to "look upon" God. In a place dedicated to worship and where there was an altar for sacrifice, David felt a nearness to God different from that felt in other locations. Our nearest equivalent to the ancient sanctuary is the church. But can we, in our search for the devotional life, expect to go into *our* sanctuary and be rewarded as was David? We hear so much of the irrelevancy of the church. We are aware that on the average only one-third of the membership of the usual local congregation takes the trouble to attend with any regularity. Books and books have been written on the piosity and otherworld-liness of the ones who do come to services. Wise men are appalled that the church is so little involved and concerned with hunger, war, racial inequality, and other issues of the world. If these critics present a true picture of our church, is it possible to go there and find the glory of God filling the temple?

Lately there has been some rethinking of those weaknesses, and writers from various schools of theological thought agree that while the church must struggle prodigiously to over-come the faults mentioned, it must not neglect the source of the power required to make the changes; it must remember that "man does not live by bread alone"; it must re-assume its unique mission of being the means of grace to mankind.

Even as we recognize the imperfections of the church, we also realize that to men it must be the place of the presence of God. Each one of us who goes and comes in the church for the express purpose of humbly seeking will contribute to the total devotional life of the church and will bring it back to God's intentions.

Thanking David for the footprints he has left for us to follow along the road to God, we go on to inquire of others. Cornelius and Peter found out something that we need to know, and the account of that is related in the tenth chapter of the Acts.

Achievement marks the devotional

The experience of Cornelius and Peter demonstrates that a devotional life is not exempt from the practical question: "What does it do?" We shall see that a devotional life is more than an inner, mystical state that never demonstrates a power outwardly.

In the first place Cornelius *proved* that he was a man of devotion by doing something for the needy in his vicinity; he was known as one who gave alms to the poor. He prayed for others, then fortified his prayers by sacrificial deeds.

His example spoke both to the godly and ungodly and they marked him down as a "God-fearer" or worshiper.

One day as Cornelius was engaged in what we call "devotional exercises," he had a vision and heard a voice. Mystics speak of this kind of revelation as "guidance." Cornelius was led to send servants to the city of Joppa to seek out a man called Peter. In our investigation of the devotional life we are helped if we note that this vision and leading came as a result of prayers *and* acts of charity; Cornelius's twofold devotional life of inner and outer obedience to God brought him along on a progressive step toward his Creator.

All men equal before God

While Cornelius was having his exalted experience and guidance, Peter in Joppa, in his turn, was having a vision as he prayed. But his vision was strange and unwelcome because he was shown creatures that his training had taught him to consider filthy and untouchable. Peter was told to prepare and eat these unclean creatures inasmuch as nothing that God has made is to be considered unclean or unworthy. This vision prepared Peter for the messengers of Cornelius and impelled him to accept their invitation to eat in the house of, to him, an "unclean" Gentile.

Remembering our examination of the church, we grieve that there are members and entire congregations who balk at bringing into the fold people of other races and nationalities. If a church is engaged earnestly in a devotional life, will not God give to that church the vision granted to Peter that all life created by God is of equal value and is not to be despised or spurned?

Devotion draws people together

Peter and Cornelius did not have nationality in common, but they did have a common experience; they were both seeking God. And this experience brought them together so that they might share with each other what they knew of God. Peter spoke to Cornelius, his family, and neighbors of the new revelation of God that had been brought by Jesus, and all who heard made a great step upward in the devotional life. This raises a point for our thought: If enough Christians cultivate a deep devotional life and these Christians are to be found in all parts of the world (as we know them to be), cannot we hope that nations will come together bound in a common purpose for righteousness? May we not believe that there are seeking Christians in China, in Russia, in all the Iron Curtain countries, and in all Asia, Africa, India, and South America? If daily the prayers of these unknown people are matching our intercessions, as Peter and Cornelius were matching theirs, cannot we hope to be brought together to change the world?

Where do we stand?

Have we begun to discover the awesome and gladsome nearness of God available through the devotional life? Have we come to a definition of the devotional life and found some paths into it? If at least we have discovered our great need for a deeper fellowship with God, then we are on the way.

PRAYER PATTERN: God my Father, I have been told and have read that you are closer to me than my very breathing and nearer even than my hands or feet; now that is becoming a reality as I see the beginning of a path to you in my inner self. Help me, I pray, to a greater effort toward awareness of you. Amen.

2

The Bible Trail to God

Starting Points: Psalm 119:9-18, 97-104; 2 Timothy 3:14-17.

How difficult to listen! Talking seems so much more fun! Yet listening is one of the essentials of the devotional life. Unless we can learn to listen as we search for God, we may find on the trail a solid wall between ourselves and the divine.

Where can we go to be within hearing distance of God's voice and work? As we go on in our study of the devotional life, we shall be looking at a number of possibilities for hearing God, but in this chapter we are to look again at a tried and true location, the Bible. Many men, women, and young people of countless generations have had reason to speak of the Bible as "the Word of God." His voice is heard as he speaks to men in the Old and New Testaments.

Our inspired "Holy Book"

All major religions have books that contain the message of their god, their Holy Books. The Hindus have the Vedas, the Mohammedans the Koran, the Mormons the Book of Mormon, the followers of Confucius his Sayings; the Jews have the Old Testament, and the Christians have taken the Old Testament and added to it the New. Why do we who call ourselves followers of the Christ insist that it is in *our*

15

Bible that God proclaims his eternal truths? Why do we not dwell on the Koran, for instance? In answer, we speak of *our* Bible as being "inspired."

For the sake of a confident devotional life we need to examine the term "inspiration." Some of us may agree with our forefathers who received every word in the Bible as literally inspired of God in the way that a man dictates exact words to his secretary. Others of us may find some difficulty with this approach.

At the outset we know that the original manuscripts of the books of the Bible cannot be found and what we have now to work with are copies of copies. We know also that from these copies in Hebrew, Greek, Aramaic, and Latin we have had to make translations into English and other current languages of today. We know also that no two old manuscripts agree exactly and no two translations into English or other languages agree exactly. In fact, recently a publisher produced a book called *The New Testament from 26 Translations* [1] which indicates the variations in English translations and versions.

The variations should not surprise us when we know from experience how hard it is to copy another's writing exactly and how difficult to translate from one *modern* language into another, from French to English, for example, and have the words mean the same to a man in Paris and one in New York.

In addition, words change in meaning through the years. In the King James Version (Mark 10:14) we read "suffer": "Suffer the little children to come unto me." We need to do some research to find that "suffer" in the days of King James meant "permit" or "let." In First Thessalonians (4:15) we are surprised to find "prevent": ". . . we which are alive and remain unto the coming of the Lord shall not prevent them which are asleep." Here again we need to ferret out the fact that "prevent" was used in earlier days to mean "come

[1] Curtis Vaughan, *The New Testament from 26 Translations* (Grand Rapids, Mich.: Zondervan Publishing House, 1967).

before." These are but two examples of many that could be cited. In our day we are discovering that our boys and girls are putting new meanings to some of our words. Language will not stand still.

All this speaks of miracle! That the Bible should have gone through so many copyings and so many translations into so many languages and should have survived all the changes in the use of words to speak to us with an unaltered message is nothing less than miraculous! The inspiration is of the Spirit rather than of the letter.

With confidence, then, we go to the Bible, our Holy Book, to find God and to listen to his work and word.

Our need for the Bible message

Both the writer of Psalm 119 and the young man Timothy (as counseled by Paul in Second Timothy) found that God's word spoke to their life needs. The same can be true of us today. Many things happen to us that, from the standpoint of present human knowledge, are unexplainable and seemingly incurable. In addition to stubborn physical ills, we experience mental and physical torments peculiar to the tensions of this century. Even our astounding scientific advances can offer nothing but sedatives and advice.

This failure of human resources was illustrated strikingly in a church forum on drug addiction. Young people had been invited to attend and share their thoughts. After much discussion on instruction in the harm of using drugs, counseling for those who had fallen into the habit of drug use, and a survey of available church facilities for these and other efforts, a teenage girl spoke up: "We know more about drugs than any of you here; more classes will not help. And warnings have no effect. Our trouble is inside us." She had the answer. With all our difficulties, the trouble is not so much in ignorance as in wrong motivation. Each of us has a deep need for a devotional life that will relate the healing power and love of God to our deepest needs by means of the bridge of the Scriptures.

Others and the Bible

As we put a first hesitant foot on this trail of the Bible, we may be helped by knowing how others have found their way into the "holy of holies." Maps of spiritual journeys can be just as helpful to our spiritual lives as road maps are to physical exploration. Books and pamphlets written to guide in daily "devotions" are not to be used as rituals or crutches but as "thought starters." There may be times when we cannot seem to make progress in our search for God. We may be like a car that will not start; but with cables attached to its battery and that of another car which runs, the stalled car receives enough power to go on its own power. It may outrun the car that started it. To follow the adventures of some godly man or woman in his or her struggle with the Word of God cannot be other than beneficial. We shall come to know with others, as with the writer of Psalm 119, that in the Bible are riches greater than any the world holds and wisdom surpassing all of mankind's collected knowledge.

Reading with an open mind

We might well acknowledge at this point that all of us will be tempted to listen to the Bible for what we want to hear and to look into the Bible for what we want to see; we will try to find verification of our own preconceived notions and prejudices. King Ahab, we remember, pretended to seek the word of the Lord, but when that word came through the one honest prophet, the king refused to accept it and persecuted the one who had told the truth (1 Kings 22). In Jesus' day many of the Pharisee class refused his application of the Old Testament because they found themselves shown as persons in need of change. If we are ready to listen to God, we must be patient, honest, and purposeful. Writing to Timothy, Paul points out that Scripture is useful "for reproof, for correction." In the Greek the word "correction" may mean "set up straight."

In our devotional study of the Bible, then, we must be prepared to find much that will chastise us and set us up straight.

Reading selectively

Both the psalmist and Paul remind us that the Scriptures have many uses and are rich in insight and guidance possibilities. The Bible touches life at so many points that a reader is justified in trying to match a hurt point of his life, a confused point, an arrogant point with the Scripture passages that relate to that spot particularly. For one who is seeking an understanding of God's great dealings with man from the beginning of time, the historical books and the Acts are good, but for one bereaved these would not be the best. A bereaved person might better look to Jesus' words to Martha at the grave of Lazarus, and to Paul's words to the Corinthians in the resurrection verses. And so it goes! Almost always, a man or woman or young person will seek to satisfy definite needs as he or she finds opportunities for cultivating the devotional life. A crying need for life direction, for forgiveness, for wisdom in handling a taut family problem, for overcoming depression, for strength in weariness, for an assurance of divine love, and for security will call for specific help. The mind and heart will be tuned to listen to answers affecting the urgent concerns of the day.

Certainly, using the Bible in a slavish way will cause us to miss the very message that God intends for us; we might well fail to get the current and immediate comfort required. On the other hand, a haphazard method of using the Bible is just as bad as the inflexible routine. To open the Bible at random will rarely put us in touch with the personal quality of Scriptures.

Both the routine reading and the haphazard flipping of pages may be avoided by a basic knowledge of the makeup of the Bible and the main thrust of its various books. Time will be well spent in an effort to become acquainted thoroughly with what the Bible has to offer, and a general survey will be a permanent investment for our devotional reading. We shall be prepared to find daily messages we sorely need for the understanding and solution of whatever problem is at hand.

Bible central in devotional life

So far two facts have come to us: God is able and willing to give us light on our path, and we have urgent need for such light. Since the Bible bridges the gap between these two facts, it must be considered central in a triumphant devotional life. We might think of the Bible as a decompression chamber. After a diver has been at great depths in the ocean and has been subject to a pressure very much greater than that of his normal existence, he must be brought to the surface slowly and be put in a pressurized room or cylinder where he can be returned to the ordinary pressure of the place where he lives. As we come to the devotional life fresh from the pressures of work and worry, ecstasy and sin, and impinging human relationships, the Bible serves as a gentle initiator into the strangely different atmosphere of the presence of God. A stubborn will brought to the Bible may be transformed into submissiveness, pride to humility, anger to forgiveness, tiredness to strength, and hate to love. As we begin to sense that we are in the atmosphere of the presence of God, we shall rejoice that we have the privilege of listening to him. The Bible is the great preparer of souls for the tremendous blessings that can be received at the hands of God.

The Bible becomes part of us

Psalm 119 reveals to us the thought that words from the Bible may be "laid up" like money in a bank savings fund for future use. At the scene of his temptation, Jesus had in his being the words of God and brought them out to defeat the propositions of his tempter. In our great emergencies at the office desk, in the classroom, in man-woman relationships, over the kitchen stove, on a stretcher being rolled into an operating room, upon receiving bad news, words of God stored up through the years will come back to us in a flash to fortify us for what we must do and bear. Memorization, either deliberate or involuntary, can make the treasures of the Bible readily available.

Studied and learned, the Bible is our text for the spiritual and material life that is ours. As we have seen in Second Timothy, a knowledge of the Word of God is our basic preparation for witnessing for God in this world. Being thoroughly grounded in the Scriptures, a man or woman may go out confidently to live and speak as one who sees beyond the resources of this present world. Just as a would-be doctor must study medicine, a would-be lawyer must study law, and a would-be chemist must study chemistry, so we who are would-be children of God must study the Bible as our guide into his presence.

Which translation?

Of all the translations of the Bible, which will give to us what we have been seeking? The various versions and translations are in basic agreement as to what God has done and said. Each person must decide which of the available editions speaks to him in his language. It may be that one translation will be used for beauty of language; another will be used for its notes and scholarly exposition; yet another may be used for its orderly presentation of chapters and verses. In any event, how can we doubt that God ever speaks in the Bible and out of the Bible to anyone who will come with a readiness to listen?

PRAYER PATTERN: May your Word, Lord, be a steady light on my path and a constant lantern to guide my footsteps on the trail into your presence. Amen.

3

Approaching God in Prayer

Starting Point: Matthew 6:1-15.

"Go ahead and talk," commanded the psychiatrist.

"But," the patient objected, "I don't know what to say."

Many of us meet this kind of impasse when we approach the matter of prayer. From our study of the Bible we know that we are commanded and invited to pray, but we are not sure how to communicate with God in prayer. Just as the psychiatrist's patient had much bottled up that she wanted desperately to make known to her doctor but could not put into words, so we are aware of problems, worries, sins, and joys without number that we long to talk over with God but we cannot find the words.

Right here is, possibly, the chief misunderstanding that we have concerning prayer. From infancy when at bedtime many of us glibly repeated, "Now I lay me down to sleep . . ." and when as youths and adults we (as glibly) recited, "Our Father who art in heaven . . ." words have seemed to be the prayer. But words are, at best, only the shell of a prayer and are completely optional. Here in our study of the devotional life a closer look at prayer is required.

What is prayer?

Profitably we may begin by listening to six men who have

asked themselves, "What is prayer?" and have discovered some answers.

James Montgomery:	Prayer is the soul's sincere desire, Unuttered or expressed, The motion of a hidden fire That trembles in the breast.
Francois de Fénelon:	True prayer is nothing else than the love of God. [1]
R. C. Trench:	We must not conceive of prayer as an overcoming of God's resistance, but as a laying hold of his highest willingness. [2]
John Heuss:	The act of praying is more analogous to clearing away the underbrush which shuts out a view than it is to begging in the street. [3]
John Burnaby:	To pray is to open the heart to the entry of love—to ask God in; and where God is truly wanted, he will always come. [4]
Harry Emerson Fosdick:	For prayer is neither chiefly begging for things, nor is it merely self-communion; it is that loftiest experience within the reach of any soul, communion with God. [5]

We know, for ourselves, that prayer has something to do with that inner longing of ours to reach to the unseen world beyond us and to God who, for some definite purpose, created us. We must be prepared to accept the fact that no man, woman, or young person has yet come to the whole truth about prayer. Prayer is such a marvelous privilege that we only can hope to learn more about it each time we pray.

Preparation for prayer

May we assume that we have cast aside any thought that prayer can be put within boundaries or cast in a particular

[1] Francois de Fénelon, *Spiritual Letters,* as quoted in Robert and Mary Leavens, eds., *Great Companions* (Boston: Beacon Press, 1946), vol. 2, p. 421.

[2] As quoted in Harry Emerson Fosdick, *The Meaning of Prayer* (Philadelphia: The American Baptist Publication Society, 1915), p. 63.

[3] John Heuss, *Our Christian Vocation* (New York: The Seabury Press, Inc., 1955), p. 87.

[4] A. R. Vidler, ed., *Soundings* (London: Cambridge University Press, 1962), p. 233.

[5] Harry Emerson Fosdick, *op. cit.,* p. 32.

mold? Are we convinced that we may engage in prayer while kneeling, sitting, standing, or lying down? Have we found that we pray with our eyes open as well as shut? Have we given up the thought that we must be in a set-aside place (such as a church or upper room) to commune with God? Do we find ourselves praying while working or walking or in the bustle of life as well as in quiet, retired times? Then let us explore ways of preparing ourselves for prayer.

Several things are called to our attention in the verses from Matthew 6. One is that prayer is a personal thing concerning only the one who prays and his God. Secrecy in prayer is recommended. This does not mean we may not pray in public when the occasion requires, but that we are not to make a "show" of our prayers as a boy will do with his bicycle riding when he takes his hands from the handlebars and calls all to witness, "Look, no hands!" We are never to do anything that will say to others, "Look, I am praying!" And even within ourselves there is to be no gloating; the Scripture uses the striking expression, ". . . do not let your left hand know what your right hand is doing," or vice versa. One hand may be thought of as our sense of satisfaction over having done something praiseworthy and the other hand as our spontaneous response to God's presence. We may boast that we have followed through on a discipline of deep-breathing exercises, but do we boast of having remembered to breathe all day? Prayer is as essential and personal as breathing.

In Matthew we find a warning against heaping up "empty phrases." In our forefathers' day some church services allowed time for the Short Prayer and the Long Prayer. We may well suppose that in order to take up the allotted time the one who offered the Long Prayer had to use many, many phrases! Simplicity and directness are characteristics of a sincere prayer.

We find also in this passage from Matthew the words of the Lord's Prayer, or, as some prefer to term it, the Model Prayer. In that pattern for prayer the word "daily" is nota-

24

ble, "Give us this day our *daily* bread." In preparing for prayer it is well to note that we are not permitted to get our praying done "in advance." Praying is for the needs of the day and not for the needs of days ahead. We walk and talk with God rather than come to him for supplies once a week or once a month.

Finally, we are reminded that it is useless to pray selfishly for good that we do not intend to share with others. Take forgiveness, for example. Before we can come to prayer with any hope of being accepted and answered by God, we must be filled with willingness to forgive our brothers and sisters anything that they may have done to us.

Elements of prayer

As we prepare for prayer, we must understand that prayers vary as to content and intent. The moment of prayer determines what the prayer will be. This explains the difficulty of using written and/or printed prayers. At the time when the original author of such a prayer put down his thoughts and supplications, the prayer was his and genuine. But to take up such a prayer and endeavor to fit it to the present needs and longings is often not successful. Even so, there are some elements that occur regularly in prayers.

Adoration of God or expressed awe in his presence is surely one ingredient not to be overlooked. In the Bible we find classic examples of this. The young Isaiah, caught up in the knowledge of God's presence, heard cries of "Holy, holy, holy is the Lord of hosts" (Isaiah 6:3). And David, looking at the star-filled sky, exclaimed, "O Lord, our Lord, how majestic is thy name in all the earth!" (Psalm 8:1). If something of this quivering feeling does not come to us in prayer, perhaps we should examine ourselves to see whether or not we are in the divine presence.

Confession is a natural result of adoration. No sooner had Isaiah sensed the presence of God than he confessed immediately, "I am a man of unclean lips" (Isaiah 6:5). The great contrast between God and man, when seen, must call forth a spontaneous confession. We may well suppose that if the Pharisee mentioned in the New Testament had had even a slight vision of God's glory as compared to man's imperfection, he could not have smugly told God, "I thank thee that I am not like other men, extortioners. . . . I fast twice a week" (Luke 18:9-14).

A third factor in prayer is *thanksgiving*. Just as we set aside a holiday in November for Thanksgiving, so we are tempted to set aside special times of thanking God for all his benefits. But if his benefits are constant, should not thanksgiving be constant? As a good beginning, we might well start with gratitude for the wonderful privilege of prayer. To think that the God who has created all things great and small has made provision for us to get in touch with him!

We go on now to *intercession*. Intercession can be thought of as our willingness to stand between others and a tragedy that is about to befall them. There are two kinds of intercession. The first may be illustrated by something done by Dr. Samuel Johnson in England in the eighteenth century. A clergyman whom he knew had been condemned to death by hanging. Johnson wrote letters to prominent people on behalf of the prisoner and wrote speeches for the prisoner to read to his jailers and judges. But when all efforts failed and the man was hanged, Johnson took it quite philosophically. The other kind of intercession is that of Moses who came down from having communed with God on the mountain only to find that the people had sinned a sin that would bring them death at God's hand. When Moses sensed the imminent and deserved peril, he cried to God, ". . . forgive their sin — and if not, blot me, I pray thee, out of thy book which thou hast written" (Exodus 32:32). To intercede earnestly requires a real sharing in the woes of mankind and an unhypocritical readiness, if necessary, to suffer in the place of others.

Finally we come to what most of us too often make the major element in prayer, *petition*. There is a place for petition. God has made us dependent upon material things for life and upon balanced emotional circumstances for mental health, and he has not forgotten this "dust" part of us. In the Lord's Prayer Jesus includes "daily bread." Petition, however, is more for enablement than for selfish sufficiency. To pray for the opportunity to obtain what we need to keep us in strength and health for the Lord's work in the world is well and good. But petition for advantage that will mean that others may lack while we are favored surely has no place in prayer. To pray that all the farms in the world may have sufficient rain is good, but to have concern only for our farm and pray that it may be watered is evil.

Shall we pray?

With all the definitions of prayer, ways of preparing for prayer, and the elements of prayer before us, shall we engage in prayer? Or is prayer still an unproved experience in life? Other life functions can be tested out. If we don't eat, we starve; if we don't drink, we die of thirst; or if we don't breathe, we cease to be. If we cover our eyes, the world becomes a dark blank. If we stop our ears, we do not know music or the sounds around us that warn and guide us. But who knows whether or not prayer achieves something essential to life?

No prayerless life

In answer to our question (if we really have a question) as to whether or not prayer is an indifferent matter of choice, we might go back to our starting topic: Approaching God in Prayer. If there is value in finding God, then prayer is more life-giving than all the functions we have mentioned. God is our sustainer. We read in Genesis of the beginning of things and note that Adam did not rise nor was he put in his Eden until God breathed into him the breath of life (Genesis 2:7). Adam had all the physical and mental parts and around him was food and water in abundance, but life began only when God gave him that extra something that can come from no other source. We shall find that we have only a token existence until we are in touch with God; prayer puts us in touch.

Truly this need for God is instinctive. A person may think he is proof against prayer when all goes well, but in an emergency of danger, pain, or great grief he will cry out without thinking to a power beyond this present world.

We find in the Bible, in secular biographies, and among our family and acquaintances people who in life exhibit a plus of contentment, assurance, courage, commitment, and real zest of living because they have been or are people of prayer. The final test is to enter faithfully into a discipline of prayer in a devotional life and see what happens to us. Many of us have already had such blessings that we would never turn back, but we seek an even greater knowledge of how to pray in a way pleasing to God our Father.

PRAYER PATTERN: Lord, teach me to pray! Help me to put aside all formalities and presumptions and approach you in prayer with faith like that of a beloved child coming to his parent in perfect trust that he will not be refused comfort and help. Amen.

4
True Security Found in God

Starting Points: Psalms 57; 90:13-17; Isaiah 6:15; Romans 8:28-39.

"Safe at last!" cried out a black man standing at the entrance of Grand Central Terminal in New York City, and he stretched out his arms as if to embrace the city. I wondered to myself what he could call safety in a metropolis as full of peril and sin as New York City. But this was at a time when demonstrations in some southern states had resulted in brutal confrontations between the races, and I supposed that he might have escaped from such an encounter. In any event, he had his idea of security and I could not enter into his feelings without knowing what he had left behind him. For my part, I was about to board a train to return from that city of noise and tumult to my home in a small upstate city and I was thinking how much more secure I would feel when I got there! As we delve into the subject of security found in God, we will need to decide what is that true security which is the same for every person in the world.

Hunger for security

The hunger for security is nothing to be ashamed of; it is built into human nature just as are the hungers for food, drink, companionship, and achievement. God does not condemn this hunger but recognizes it in his promises to his children. Jesus in a synagogue read a passage from Isaiah that sums up these promises of security: "The Spirit of the Lord is upon me, because he has anointed me to preach good news to the poor. He has sent me to proclaim release to the captives and recovering of sight to the blind, to set at liberty those who are oppressed, to proclaim the acceptable year of the Lord" (Isaiah 61:1 as restated in Luke 4:18). Jesus also spoke to his followers one day in regard to their anxiety for provision of food and drink. He told them that this was the concern of all nations: "Your Father knows that you need them" (Luke 12:30). We may be sure that God does not condemn us for seeking to provide creature needs.

However, in our devotional life we can be given an understanding of the priorities of security.

Kinds of insecurity

The fundamental facts of life have not changed since the days of the writers of the Psalms, Isaiah, and Romans. In the "Starting Points" selections these men note some kinds of insecurity that beset them. Let us see if we find in the list from Psalms and Isaiah something that describes our own predicament today.

In Psalm 57 we read of "storms of destruction," adversaries that seem lionlike, a net to snare a person, and a pit to fall in. Psalm 90 speaks of the insecurity of a person who looks at his life work and wonders if it will be established. The Isaiah verses show us the dismay of a young man who suddenly is gripped by the guilt of "unclean lips."

In the Romans selection, Paul catalogs all the possible insecurities of his life:

tribulation	the troubles that fill life from end to end
distress	the anxiety for oneself and others
persecution	the harm that comes from others
famine and nakedness	times of poverty
peril	the dangers of life's journey

sword	whatever threatens life
death	the end of earthly existence
life	with its crying needs and temptations
angels	good things, privilege that lulls one to forgetfulness
principalities	the darkness of fears and depression
things present	all the glamour and drag of this world
things to come	the unknown future with possible punishment
powers	earthly and spiritual
height	the "high" that we get from pride and praise
depth	despondency and despair
anything else	whatever Paul may have missed in his list!

Insecurities peculiar to today

We know that to every generation come peculiar expressions of all the basic insecurities that man has always known. Some of the insecurities of our fathers vanish, such as extremely high infant mortality, danger in childbirth, crippling from polio, and short life span, while others of our very own come to plague us.

As we look at our world today, we find ourselves made insecure by the danger of a nuclear war, overpopulation, the seeming impossibility of keeping the peace in all parts of the world, growing drug addiction, slavery to nicotine and alcohol, loose morality, and a stubborn racism that festers more and more. Added to these nightmares, we have a job insecurity brought on by technology, the rivalry of once backward nations in the field of manufacturing, changing demands that make skills of many kinds unwanted in the market, and pollution of natural resources.

Apart from the causes of insecurity found in the material world, the sensitive find that poor communication between parents and children, irreligion, and the weakness of the churches make for gnawing insecurity.

31

What kind of security do we want?

No doubt each of us has some special insecurities that he or she would want to list, but for the most part we likely would ask for security from want of food, water, clothing, and shelter; security from the fear of war and crime; security from the ravages of painful diseases; security from a dependent old age. Given an assurance that we could depend upon all those desires being fulfilled, what else could we ask? These are the privileges that government strives to obtain for its people expressed in such terms as guaranteed annual income. Do we think, however, that people blessed with all these benefits would, as a result, be happy and friendly?

Recently someone, in an article or column, pointed out that the obvious woes are not always the worst ones. That writer suggested that an inmate of an institution for mental and emotional disorders would gladly exchange his inner turmoil for a simple case of arthritis and consider that his suffering in his new condition was much less than the awful imaginations of his former state.

It is for depth security that a person turns to God.

Security from God

In the Middle Ages thousands of men and women flocked into monasteries and nunneries to get away from the world and spend their days and nights in the presence of God. Few of us can do this in our time and, even if we could, we would take our inner insecurity with us. We know that we must find God where we are and while doing what we must.

The writer of Psalm 57 found security in God's steadfast love and faithfulness. When he came to a sense of God's love, he knew it was the kind that would never let him go; he came to know that God was faith-keeping and that none of his promises of comfort and care had ever been voided or repudiated. His trust in this kind of God became the one unchanging factor in his busy and threatened life. This assurance can be ours also, as we give ourselves to the search for the living God.

The author of Psalm 90 uses the same term for his discovery about God, "steadfast love." He finds assurance that his insecurity about his life's work can be given over to God. Quite likely he had in mind what we so often have on our minds: "What have I been doing, after all? What has been accomplished? Have I made any difference in the world?" These thoughts come at the close of a day and at retirement time. The security that came to the psalmist was what we hope and expect to find: the work was somehow God's work and, therefore, would be established forever.

When we go back to Paul with all of his cataloged miseries and fears, what do we find? Paul was reminded that God loved him enough to send his Son to die for him and this remembrance caused him to cry out that none of the things or circumstances he had mentioned could possibly separate him from that love of God; and if he could not be separated from God's love, what had he to fear?

Christian light on security

In view of what the psalmists and Paul found to their comfort, we may now consider the difference between the one who seeks security from God and the one who tries to find it in legislation, "rights," pensions, investments, psychiatric counseling, as good as these things really can be.

In the first place, the Christian begins to recognize companionship in a divine presence; he is not all alone as he faces the disastrous conditions that surround him. He feels the force of Christ's promise, "I am with you always" (Matthew 28:20). The story of the three young men who were shoved into an extremely hot furnace (Daniel 3) becomes our story. They walked in the heat and flames and did not die, and the astounded king who had them cast into the furnace exclaimed, "Did we not cast three men bound into the fire? . . . But I see four men loose, walking in the midst of the fire, and they are not hurt; and the appearance of the fourth is like a son of the gods" (Daniel 3:24-25). We shall find the strength and courage to endure our fiery trials without being bound by them or consumed since God becomes one with us.

A second consideration for the Christian is that he has a new vision of what real security is. If security has meant for us physical life, health, family accord, safety, and steady work, we shall see that these are comparatively small things. True security will come to us in terms of divine forgiveness, inner strength to bear all things, the opportunity for serving our fellowman and an unshakable faith in community of life in God's presence.

For the Christian, a third consideration is that anxiety is a wall against security, and that the anxious person will always be insecure. Today is to be the unit of life, not tomorrow. If God gives us a tomorrow, he will give with it the security that we need. We come to peace when we come to the point of trusting God implicitly and make the body a means of life instead of the end and aim of life.

Security takes over from insecurity

When an evangelist becomes quite personal with his hearers and demands of them, "Do you want to be saved?" he is appealing to their insecurity. Who does not want to be saved in the sense of having a certainty of being with God now and forever? In this chapter we have been groping for our meaning of security and the way of coming to it by God's grace. Not all at once, perhaps, but in a growing way our insecurity will go bit by bit. We shall begin to "practice the presence of God" as did Brother Lawrence as he scrubbed the pots and pans in the kitchen of his monastery. Wherever we are and whatever honest occupation is ours, we shall feel the helping hand.

Permanence will come into our lives and bring the security that only permanence can bring. We shall realize that we are not children of God for today only but for every day that he gives us and throughout eternity. Abram lacked a sense of permanence in the defended cities of Ur and Haran but found it on a pilgrimage where things were few but God was.

After we have placed our hand in the hand of the Lord and know that the Lord is looking at the same world and the same clouds, we shall be able to face the dire problems of our world and the looming clouds without dread. And God is never dismayed; this is his world, and he loves the world and us.

PRAYER PATTERN: Father, you know that I shall falter despite my new knowledge of the true security which I have in you. Keep me steady hour after hour. Amen.

5

Faith Shows the Way

Starting Points: Job 23; 42:1-6; Hebrews 12:5-11; 1 Peter 5:6-7.

Columbus discovered a land which later was given the name "America." That land is known now around the world and anyone wanting to visit can easily find its location. But faith cannot be localized in the same way so that we or anyone may approach it at will. A scientist in his laboratory may take a fluid or a mold and separate from the mass a particular variety of bacteria. Faith cannot be so separated from all else in the world, put in a container, and labeled. A telephone lineman can take a tangled group of cables and pick out the one that is connected to the phones in a certain area. Faith cannot be so singled out in the mass of possibilities within a person's life. Faith is elusive and deserves our deep thought as we endeavor to find out what it is and whether or not we have it.

Faith understood

As we begin our search, the finding of a writer of many years ago may give us a clue:

> Faith is not the action of a separate and distinct faculty. It is the fusion of the whole mind in one supreme seizure of truth. This act is not analyzable, because it is not made up of decipherable mental processes. [1]

[1] John W. Buckham, *Personality and the Christian Ideal* (Boston: The Pilgrim Press, 1909), p. 218.

In other words we might say that faith is a total way of approaching life and determines what we do with all our faculties and gifts. We speak of food as being "wholesome," but we do not mean that wholesomeness is an ingredient as are flour, salt, sugar, or yeast. Wholesomeness is a quality of each ingredient and of the whole concoction. Faith is that kind of all-pervading essence. When we speak of "a man of faith," do we mean that everything that makes up the man plus his words and deeds illustrates a certain motivation?

To narrow our search even more, we are now seeking to understand the faith that is the gift of God. We shall try to comprehend the difference that faith makes in our lives.

Faith asks, "Why?"

We go far afield when we think that faith must be thought of as "unquestioning." The very fact that faith includes continual visions of what might be changed in the world to bring in the kingdom of God provides for questioning. Although the whole Bible is a book of faith and the word "faith" jumps out at us from every nook and cranny, the Bible contains many instances of questioning that came because of faith. No one can throw a question at God without having faith that God is.

Job is a standard example of the questioning man of faith. One of his questions is sometimes ours: "Oh, that I knew where I might find him" (Job 23:3). Concerning God he is asking, "Where is he?" Are we not doing the same in our private devotions when we cannot seem to "get through" to God? In our many conferences, discussions, and books, do we not find that same question back of all the theology and speculation?

A second question of Job is most pertinent to our condition: "Why are not times of judgment kept by the Almighty, and why do those who know him never see his days?" (Job 24:1). When we see little children who have been burned with napalm, when we read of fine young people victimized by drug-pushers until their lives are ruined, when we consider how black men, American Indians, and Mexican Americans are cruelly exploited and despised, do we not wonder, "Why does God permit all this?"

Our questions can be those of a deep faith because they are directed to God in whom we believe, and through our questions we attempt to understand why a loving and just God does not stop the atrocities and horrors around us; we have faith that God abhors such deeds as foreign to his purpose for man.

Faith transforms

Job's questions — and our questions — although growing out of faith, are answered only when we find ourselves in the presence of God and when we are willing to hear him. When God appeared to Job out of the whirlwind of his doubts, Job realized that he was right to think of God as righteous and just, but that he was wrong to suppose that the sufferings of a believer indicate an uncaring God. Job found — and we will find — that suffering is possible to godly people and innocent people. The truth comes that, to a large extent, God has entrusted the "least of his brethren" to us who believe, and we are to relieve their sufferings. Faith in what God says to us will transform our whole attitude toward the evil in the world. Instead of standing off wringing our hands and wondering why God does not "do something," we go out and do something in God's name.

In thus doing something we may well be hurt. The writer of Hebrews discovered that following Christ brings more than the average of hardship and trouble into the follower's life. These tribulations are a mark of distinction; we are in the forefront of the fight for righteousness because our God depends upon us to carry the day for him; of course we are in danger of wounds. The transformation that faith makes in a life is something like this: Job sat in the ashes after the messengers had brought news of the death of his children and the loss of his flocks and herds. He suffered and bemoaned the fact that God was not taking vengeance

on those who were taking advantage of the poor and innocent.

After faith laid hold, Job rose up, shook off the ashes,
and took charge of his affairs. His new sense of God's greatness may even have undergirded him in taking an active role
in rebuilding his life. In our day, we may be too ready to content ourselves in reading the dire reports of awful happen-
ings in the world and asking why God does nothing. Faith
shows us that God does nothing because his troops refuse
to leave their fortified positions while his other children
are being ravished. And then we rise up to do what can be
done in the strength of God. There was a time in England
and America when pastors and people felt that they were
doing their share in the salvation of the world by praying
specifically and long for the salvation of all the heathen.
Then William Carey and Adoniram Judson and others received by faith the vision that the heathen would be saved
only when Christians went to them with the Good News.

Faith entrusts

Turning to a lesson of faith that came to Peter, we find
that we as Christians have a method of handling our burdens
and the burdens of our brothers that the unbeliever does not
have. In brief this is the invitation of God to "Cast all your
anxieties on him, for he cares about you" (1 Peter 5:7; see
also Psalm 55:22). This does not mean that we go scot-free.
We might think of how we cast our physical problems onto our
doctor because he is the one who understands them and who
can dose us, operate on the diseased part, prescribe disciplines, and show us how to live at our best with what cannot
be cured. And we might think of how we cast all our legal
concerns on our lawyer because he is the one who understands them and can guide us through the tangles of the law.
We could look at this in other areas of life: we take our
ignorance of certain subjects to a teacher, our financial
needs to a banker, our housing problems to a real estate
broker. Note that we do not get rid of medical, legal, edu-

cational, financial, and other anxieties, but we do have the assurance that we have had the best advice and help, that someone is taking an interest in our problems. So do we cast our burdens on the Lord who knows all about them and can give us guidance and peace. We remember that Paul had some disability that he called his "thorn in the flesh" and he cast this on the Lord many times; the disability did not go away, but Paul had the comfort of knowing that God was using that defect to make him strong.

We must first experience humility before we realize our need for God and are willing to turn in faith to him with our cares. The pride in self that says, "I can handle all my affairs without outside help," does not permit our turning to the Lord. This kind of pride exercised in other departments of life would exclude the help of the doctor, lawyer, teacher, and others and would bring great catastrophes upon a person. We may be sure that the greater the faith we have in God, the more humble we shall be in admitting that we are not sufficient to do everything alone.

Faith discloses meaning

Faith does not "give" meaning to events but it discloses the meaning that is there already. God has placed a meaning upon everything. Only by faith is the meaning shown.

Going back to Job and looking at him again in his sackcloth and ashes rubbing his sores, we see a man who could not sense any meaning in all this. Eventually by faith he saw a meaning. This unhappy climax to his life was to bring him out of pride and self-sufficiency and the conviction that he, as a righteous man, could do no wrong, to a state of utter dependence upon God and to the point where he could experience God's presence. Ritualism in Job's life gave way to an intimate relationship with God. This is the kind of change that we hope to see in our lives as we ponder faith in our devotional character.

For Job's ashes and boils each of us can substitute something equally disturbing and for which we must see meaning.

Among the circle of the readers of this chapter there may well be divorce in the family, children on drugs or living outside of marriage, cancer or other incurable disease, uncertain financial undergirding, youthful disillusionment with the Establishment, betrayed love, guilt over sin, and hundreds of other soul-shaking anxieties. Added to these will always be the ills of the world, each of which affects us to a real extent. Now what is the meaning in these cares?

When we give ourselves over to God as did Job and the writers of Hebrews and Peter and when we feel faith taking hold, meaning will emerge and we shall be comforted.

Meaning begins to appear the moment we come to the knowledge that God cares for us. The most desolate person of any age is the one who is convinced that "nobody cares." If we will not accept God's assurance that he cares for us, how can we forget his act of sending his Son to go to the cross for *our* sins? When we come in our devotional life to the place of being able to say of God as did Job, "My eye sees thee," then meaning is near.

Meaning is still nearer when we go so far as to exchange our "if" faith for a "no matter what" faith. We remember how Thomas, the disciple, speaking of the resurrection, said, "Unless I see in his hands the print of the nails, and place my finger in the mark of the nails, and place my hand in his side, I will not believe." (See John 20:25.) We might say much the same and offer our belief in the meaning of things only when we see a miracle putting an end to our disease or causing a war to cease. Without overworking Job, let us learn from him that he accepted his fate while yet in his misery and before God had restored fortune and health to him. We shall be able to see meaning if we are able to face life knowing that what troubles us may never be any better outwardly. If our cares were easily reversible, what would be the purpose in their occurring to us?

Going a bit further, each of us can be helped to meaning by remembering that he is but one of the billions of God's children. The great laws of creation keep us fixed to a stable world. When darkness surrounds us, we know that that means there is light shining on others. When we have rain, some are enjoying clear weather elsewhere. In human behavior and its results, good deeds benefit both good and evil men; evil deeds hurt both good and evil men. Some of our difficulties come because we are "innocent bystanders" in the vast operations of a world of people. Faith will show us that evil has not been "sent" upon us by God, but that God can and will make meaningful to our life whatever comes.

A conclusion

Perhaps now we have a picture of what we were groping toward, a meaningful faith. By giving ourselves over without reservation to God and waiting patiently for him, by refusing to consider our troubles as divine punishment, by not seeking quick remedies for our ills, by practicing the throwing of *all* our concerns and the concerns of our brothers on God, we have hope of coming to the steady experience of the "everlasting mercy" and the "steadfast love" of God.

Then when we have found meaning for our own despairs and trials, we shall be ready to go out and speak of comfort to our fellowman. We may be as Joseph. When his brothers sold him into slavery, he did not want to change his position as the favored son of his doting father; but when he settled down as a slave in Egypt, he used that bondage to save the lives of his brothers and father. Faith can bring us to the great calmness and sense of purpose that came to Paul: "Not that I complain of want; for I have learned, in whatever state I am, to be content" (Philippians 4:11). This kind of faith can be ours as we persevere in the cultivation of a deep devotional life.

PRAYER PATTERN: Lord, you know that I prefer not to be handicapped as I am, but I am leaving all this to you. If my agonies and worries must remain, show me the hidden meaning; if my cares go from me, keep me from lack of understanding of my suffering brothers and sisters. Amen.

6

God's Guidance

Starting Points: 1 Kings 19:9-18; John 16:7-15.

A prayer in an old hymn which we sing occasionally puts into words what we are to explore in this chapter:

> Guide me, O Thou great Jehovah,
> Pilgrim through this barren land.

Through our study of the Bible, our experience of prayer, our reaching out for security, and our strengthening grasp on faith, we have come to realize that our journey through life and to God covers strange and unfamiliar territory. A wise person who is about to go into an unknown land seeks some kind of guide.

To be of any value, a guide who is capable of leading us safely and happily through a foreign country must be one who has been through the country; a native who has spent his life there is greatly to be desired. As we look at the coming days of our life and at the life beyond this one, we dread going forward without a guide. But who is capable of taking us by the hand as we walk the precipitous roads, as we push through the jungles, as we struggle across the deserts of life? Who knows the way to eternal and triumphant life? The answer, of course, is that the guide is God; only he knows what lies ahead of us.

Need for guidance

Our urgency in looking for guidance will be in proportion to our sense of need. This awareness grows as we mature in the faith. We may remember that as children we resented being "told" or "helped." We were quite capable of doing things and finding places without adult aid! But now that we are older, we are sensible enough to know that a Tour Guide and Information Center can spare us aimless traveling and failure to find our destination. Even so with our vital journeying. Slowly we come to know how childish and disastrous is our thinking if we believe our own resourcefulness and determination are sufficient for our day-by-day push into the unknown. Every future moment is without a map; every emerging joy or sorrow, failure or success, or time of health or illness represents a new and unexperienced situation. A reliable guide is essential.

How guidance comes

In the passage from First Kings we find a man desperately in need of God's guidance, Elijah the prophet. In order to find his guide, he decided the best place to look was at a spot where the Guide had been found before. Therefore, Elijah went to Mount Horeb (also known as Mount Sinai and as "the mount of God"). He knew from the history of his forefathers that God had appeared here to Moses out of the midst of the burning bush and later to all the Israelites at the time of the giving of the law.

Elijah's action can be a hint to us. Where in the past have we felt that guidance came to us? What were we doing in our devotional life; what mood of spirit were we in; what circumstances seemed conducive to our certainty that someone was leading us? We can try to renew that former occasion. Phillips Brooks speaks of this:

Do you think that Moses will not speak of the bush, and Samuel of the little temple chamber, and Peter and John of their boats on the still lake, and Paul of the Damascus road, and Matthew of his tax table, and the poor woman of the wayside well, when they are met above? . . . It is indeed a goodly spirit that treasures its past miracles, that goes down the gracious avenues of life *to find the bushes out of which it first heard God's voice*.[1]

Elijah teaches us also that to find the Guide we must withdraw from the distractions of people and the world. Even in a crowd or in a family circle, the individual may withdraw inwardly until he is receptive only to God. As Elijah then waited for the Lord, so we must wait. There was a young woman in a circle of friends who was asked to do something. She said, "I must find out what God wants me to do about that." And she rushed off to her room. In five minutes she returned and insisted that God had given her the answer! Our Guide will not be so rushed. Our impatience is a barrier between us and the Guide. He will come when there is the need.

Elijah learned still another lesson from which we can profit. Elijah wanted God to come to him in some magnificent, terrible, and mighty fashion. He thought that an earthquake, a mighty wind, or a consuming fire would be appropriate. He had to learn that God guides with "a still small voice" (1 Kings 19:12). Or, as some scholars translate the original language, "a gentle silence." We too sometimes expect strong guidance in the form of strange events that pull or shove us in one direction or another. Instead we may not even be aware of our Guide as quietly he helps us find the path and the words for which we grope.

A proof that we are traveling under the direction of the Guide is that our feeling of loneliness disappears. A comforting feeling of companionship is ours not only because of the presence of the Guide but because we begin to realize that many others are on our road and sharing the same trials and hardships of the journey. When Elijah went to find God, he thought that he was the only one in all of the nation who wanted the true God. Then God told him

[1] H. L. S. and L. H. S., eds., *Phillips Brooks Yearbook* (New York: E. P. Dutton & Co., Inc., 1893), pp. 55, 56. Italics added.

of seven thousand others who were faithful and seeking the right way in the world.

The Spirit guide

In the verses from John, the Guide is given a name, the Holy Spirit. We are assured that this Guide will lead us into truth. "What is truth?" (John 18:38), Pilate asked Jesus as he stood before the judgment seat. Pilate seemed to classify truth along with other commodities which might be recognized and secured. But the disclosure of truth comes by the ministrations of a guide who will lead us steadily into the habitation of the true. Older people speak with some dismay of the "generation gap." But to some extent this gap is explained by the discovery of younger people that the older generation has not found the whole truth; they are seeing glimmers of more truth ahead, truth that will lead them out of war into peace, out of race prejudice into brotherhood, out of hypocrisy into sincerity, out of materialism into a life not clogged so much by "things." If these young people will trust the Spirit Guide, they will find this truth that tantalizes them now.

The Spirit Guide also deals with us on our journey by interpreting the signs along the way. What, for instance, is the direction in the statement of the Ten Commandments (Exodus 20) and in the Sermon on the Mount (Matthew 5, 6, 7)? Have we missed the pointers which could have led mankind upward to heights of living that would have been far above the violence and tragedy that explode around us in the polluted swamps where we have built our life's dwelling places?

Continuing with his guidance, the Spirit takes us on to new things. This is in contrast to the strange movement among us now to go back to the old ways. The spectacle styles of our grandfathers and grandmothers are being revived; the long hair and beards of patriarchal times seem desirable; old plays and old motion pictures are being rerun; our old national mistakes of defrauding the American Indian and enslaving the black man are coming out of the past to fan the fires of a guilt complex. It may be that some of this nostalgic movement is part of our effort to go back to where we felt we had better guidance and where life was more personal and simpler. We cannot progress by attempting to turn back the calendar. There can be no return to a nonnuclear-oriented world, to a nontechnological world. The Spirit leads us to new things which will help us use our progress for all mankind and for the glory of God. Jesus brought a freshness to life and a newness to the world that left the old behind, and the guide brings this to our remembrance.

Discovering guidelines

Since we now know that we are in constant need of God's guidance, how shall we utilize our devotional life to find the way? First of all, turning to the Scriptures is wise. To many the Bible will be the best Mount of God to which to go. We shall find definite commandments, firm pronouncements, and clear-cut instructions there. In addition, we shall find illustrations of how other men, women, and young people heeded the words of the Guide and found their way through life to a joyful journey's end. Among these will be Abraham, Isaac, Jacob, David, the psalmists, the early disciples, and others. Their cries for guidance when they were losing the way and the answers that came to them will be immensely helpful to us.

A second guideline is seeking the will of God by the help of the Spirit. Even though we see that the treasures of God's guidance are in the Bible in full measure and that there are manifold revelations in the world about us, the Spirit is needed to help us recognize these compelling truths and to show us how to apply the vast treasures to our particular needs. Consider this teacher-pupil illustration. In a class gathered for the study of a branch of mathematics, each member has in his possession a textbook. Without new knowledge he understands the numerals from 1 to 10 and he can read the instructions. But even with this knowledge he cannot begin to solve the strange problems that are set before him. The teacher will instruct him in the use of the familiar numerals and explain to him what the words he is reading are trying to tell him. Soon the pupil feels comfortable in his new subject. So it is with our use of nature, history, and the Bible; these become meaningful beyond the ABC's of germination, and the rise and fall of empires. We are shown the warnings and the pointers until they become obvious and usable.

A third guideline is supplied in the fellowship of other believers and seekers. We have been told to gather ourselves together for worship, praise, and study. Power can be experienced in the earnest prayers of a number of wayfarers who are asking for a guide. Small groups where problems can be discussed and shared and brought before the Lord provide good opportunity to hear God speak. Even on a one-to-one basis, two Christians may spark something that will lead to a better understanding of God's will.

General and specific guidance

The guidance that we seek from God will be both general and specific. Let us think of a sea captain or the pilot of an airplane. Before either one begins his journey, he needs to receive from the navigator a general course which he will follow with the aid of his compass. But when great storms come, guidance is needed for altering the course to avoid danger. Further, when a ship is entering a port or a jet plane is making a landing, special guidance is requested from a harbor pilot or an airport tower. Guidance for life is much the same; we need to be told how to chart our general life course in righteousness, and we need specific instructions when the storms of temptation, bereavement, illness, depression, and guilt blow upon us. Finally, we shall need hand-to-hand guidance when we make the landfall of death.

We will lose much if we decide, once we have found our

direction by giving ourselves to God and, perhaps, by baptism and church membership, that we have all we need. When census takers of one kind or another compile statistics about religion, one-third of the people in the world of today claim to be "Christian." Somewhere, sometime they felt that they had found that direction for life. Obviously that has failed a great proportion of them or this world would be vastly different than it is. Life's general direction may be as a traveler's "due north," but to go due north, the traveler will come to hills, rivers, cliffs, and thick woods. He will be face to face with decisions as to what detours, fordings, bypassings, and alternate routes are wise and advisable.

We shall face specific decisions when we see so much need for our talents and want to give of ourselves to the best possible advantage. Some of us will have to decide whether to endure a difficult marriage or dissolve it; others will need to know what attitudes to take toward our country's entrance into war. Many will look for guidance to deal adequately with fair housing or school bussing, or to answer questions, such as what sacrifices shall we make for the least of our brethren, or how shall we rebuild a life shattered by sin? These are times when the general direction is good, but we cry out, "What do I do now, God?"

Of one thing we may be sure: If God's guidance does not result from our devotional life, then we need to seek for a deeper fellowship with the Lord. God's children need not stumble along in the darkness since the Light of Life has shone upon men.

PRAYER PATTERN: "Guide me, O Thou great Jehovah, pilgrim through this barren land." And may your leading help to make the land less barren, even to blossom as the rose. Amen.

7

Learning to Praise the Lord

Starting Points: Psalms 103:1-5; 104; 150.

"How do I love thee? Let me count the ways."[1]

A poet wrote these words concerning her love for another, but they are appropriate for us to use as we contemplate our feelings toward God. So far in our study of the devotional life we have been concentrating on the values that may accrue to us; now we need to pause for awhile to think of at least one way that we can express our love for the Lord. Praise is one available expression of our love.

Examining praise

Praise, in general, is an act of adulation, homage, and gratitude and is an indication of the value or worth which we concede to the one being praised. Praise to God must have an added something, an inner conviction of God's matchless glory. Our praise of God will naturally be in proportion to how much God means to us; our praise can be no greater than the size of our appraisal of God.

Praise may be expressed outwardly through prayers, songs, or hymns; participation in choral arrangements; public wit-

---

[1] Elizabetth Barrett Browning, "Sonnets from the Portuguese," *The Complete Poetical Works of Elizabeth Barrett Browning* (Boston: Houghton Mifflin Company, 1900), p. 223.

nessing; and gifts of time, talent, and money to be used to God's glory. Praise may be expressed inwardly by meditating on the excellencies of God, by sincere thankfulness for blessings, or by prayers of pure exultation.

The psalmist's pattern of praise

Numerous instances of instantaneous praise and programmed praise can be found all through the Bible; the first two chapters of Luke are notable examples. In this part of Luke we find praise for the births of John and Jesus as voiced by an angel, by John's mother Elizabeth, by Mary, by John's father Zechariah and by the prophet and priest Simeon. But for variety and continuity of praise there is a richness in the Psalms not found elsewhere.

For instance, Psalm 103 is such a true hymn that words and phrases from it have found their way into hymns of the church which we use today.

The psalmist sets an example by invoking his utmost ability to praise the Lord. Every particle of his being must be given in total and absolute devotion to God. A sense of depth and quality comes through to us. Today in our churches we find the erroneous view that numbers of people, quantities of dollars, and huge sanctuaries are the measure of our praise. So, individually, we are tempted to act on the same principle. But the psalmist had learned by experience through life that praise cannot be successful without total devotion. Later, Jesus was to teach this truth to his disciples as they watched men and women bringing their gifts to the temple treasury. Many rich men came and cast in lordly sums. And then a widow came and threw in two pitiably small coins. Jesus told his followers that, of all who had come to bring offerings, this woman had given the largest amount to God. Why? Because she had put in "everything she had" (Mark 12:41-44).

The writer of Psalm 104 adds to our knowledge of praise by giving God glory as the provider for and sustainer of man's life. He stands in awe of the world that he sees around

him, filled with marvels and change and yet dependably stable. God and not man has been the initiator, and the psalmist sees God as the one and only Creator. Around us from horizon to horizon, above us as far as eye or telescope can see, or in the depths of the sea, man can come across the works of God. Perhaps in our day we are returning to this sense of appreciation of God as our astronauts come back from the moon with eyewitness accounts of the beauty and strangeness of that distant heavenly body and with rock samples so old that we stagger at the thought of the ages behind them. The moon has existed all of this time without being touched or seen close-up by man. The psalmist shows us that praise is fortified by looking around us.

In Psalm 150 we find another ingredient of praise, enthusiasm. The psalm starts out with a Hallelujah ("Praise the Lord!"). And this spirit continues until the last verse where we find a doxology that has echoed down the years. How tame and flat much of our personal and church praise seems compared to this psalm! Praise cannot come by the clock or be fitted into our small routines; praise must burst forth at any time and in any place even if we cannot express it audibly. If in our devotional life we are coming to an assurance of the nearness of God, and if we are having new visions of what God means to us, how can we resist moments when shouts of praise fairly race through our being?

God as praiseworthy

Aren't we often tempted to praise someone for what he has *done* for *us*? Does not this temptation extend to our praise of God? We noted in the harsh experiences of Job that he decided to praise God in spite of all his troubles. Yet, we cannot help but recognize the gifts of God. However, our praise should be for the love of God that prompted him to be so bountiful to us rather than for the gifts themselves. First, then, shall we look at some of the things God has done?

The psalmist began by praising God for his gifts in nature which brought to man beauty, food, clothing, shelter, and the materials for all scientific advance and cultural progress. Man, as we remember, came to the world with nothing but the life that God gave him, and he found in the world which God had made, everything that he has today.

When the writer of Psalm 103 listed the "benefits" he received from God, he did not go into houses and lands and jewels and cattle; he mentioned forgiveness, healing, redemption, love, and mercy — all things that brought good, youthlike vitality. He recalled deliverance from danger.

In our day of increasing population, we are brought to a soul-shaking realization of the immensity of God's provision for his children. Recently, a statistician estimated that every baby born in the early seventies would need 46,000,000 gallons of water during his lifetime. This figure was based on our current use of water in our modern conveniences as well as the use for drinking and cooking. Add to this one person's astounding demand for water the lifetime requisition for tons of food, fuel for cooking and warmth, material for clothing and housing, paper for books, magazines, newspapers, and other paper products, and steel for cars and appliances! If we multiply this by the number of expected births in one year, we know that only God with his infinite resources and powers can meet the need. History demonstrates to us that God's children have been supplied generation after generation.

Beyond our praise of God for what he gives, we find him praiseworthy for what he is. Goodness, love, mercy, forgiveness, and fatherliness we find in God. We see imperfection in ourselves and in the world, but in God we see perfection and know that what we are and what the world is can never be the norm of what life is intended to be. How could we strive for a better world except that we know what God is and what his world should be? The only thing that keeps us from utter despair is that there is a better character and a better way possible.

In our time we have additional reasons for knowing God as praiseworthy. Our young people are raising questions about war, poverty, and race that send us back to God's teachings in both Old and New Testaments. The preaching of God's word in the world has brought even simple, uneducated people to a knowledge of their worth, and they are struggling toward independence and dignity of life.

Aspects of vital praise

We have learned from the psalmists and we have explored the praiseworthiness of God: perhaps we are ready to inquire, with eagerness, what direction our praise may take.

Plain, old-fashioned gratitude is praise. At Christmas, after presents have been opened and the excitement has died down, we look again at the cards to learn the names of our benefactors in order to make phone calls or write notes expressing our thanks for the remembrances. Sometimes it happens that a card has been lost. How desolate we are because we have no way of thanking the giver! And when we examine all of the gifts that come to us in life and know how many have not come from the hand of man, should we not hurry to thank our God? How incomplete life would be without an outlet of thankful return for unearned benefits!

A second aspect of praise is joy. We have noted the contagious joy in Psalm 150. The recurring thought of what God is and that he is ever mindful of his children is enough to fill our hearts with a joy that must have expression. One of the greatest errors of some of our forefathers was that they thought religion was a department of life that was to be kept somber and formal. This was not so in Bible times. A reading of the description of tabernacle or temple brings out the colorful appearance of the bright robes and fittings. The worship had a joyful ring. We do not sense the sadness, melancholy, and self-restraint of our modern church services and, perhaps, of our personal devotions. If any of us are shocked a bit by the innovations in church services being tried by young people — the guitars, the gay lilt of the songs, the informal liturgies — we should remember perhaps how scandalized King David's wife was when she saw him dancing before the Lord! (See 2 Samuel 6:14-16.) Paul, in his day, tried to recover this spirit of joy and counseled new believers: "Rejoice in the Lord always; again I will say, Rejoice" (Philippians 4:4).

When earlier we looked at prayer, we included adoration as one part. In praise, too, there is more than a touch of adoration. We can find some of our loved ones and a few of our fellowmen who deserve our respect, even our admiration, but not one who is really good enough for adoration. Only in our praise of the deity do we find adoration in order. Praise of God reaches beyond anything we can feel for a human being and lifts us up to the One who is infinitely superior to us. Awe is involved here and is good for our souls.

Praise today

Certain days of the week and certain special days have been set aside for worship as men have experimented with ways of praising God. Customarily (but this is changing a bit now) we use Sunday as the day of the Lord and make that day one marked by praise. One other day in the week, at least, appeals to many church people as another opportunity for praise in church between sabbaths.

Thanksgiving, Christmas, the Lenten season, Easter, Pentecost, and a few other church special days cannot be thought of apart from praise to God.

A later chapter will bring more detailed thoughts on corporate praise.

But today we are coming to realize that perfected praise is the practice of living as servants in the world. To proclaim the kingdom of God in which there is no room for war; racial, national, or class discriminations; poverty; prejudice; or injustice is surely the ultimate in praise of God. We read many passages in the Bible that justify and fortify this stand. Isaiah is quite clear that his understanding of God's revelation shows that prayers and formal worship are repulsive to God if the worshiper is an oppressor of his fellowman (among other verses we find this in Isaiah 1:12-17). Jesus makes the same point when he tells us that a gift is not to be offered by one who is not at peace with his brother (Matthew 5:23-24).

One conclusion that comes to us as we think of praise as part of our devotional life is that praise is a privilege, yes, a reward, that comes in the midst of life to elevate us for a moment on some personal or community Mount of Transfiguration for the purpose of giving us strength for the work below. Praise is to us what a sudden ray of sunshine is to a drab and dreary day.

PRAYER PATTERN: Dear Father God, may my spirit break loose from its bindings of the commonplace and proper and give way for a glad Hallelujah! Amen.

8

Confession for Forgiveness

Starting Points: 2 Samuel 12:1-15; Psalm 51; 1 John 1:8-9.

Looking pointedly at a pupil in the fourth row, a teacher said, "You are getting very careless in your lesson preparation."

Automatically, the boy turned and looked at the person behind him because he could not believe that he had done anything blameworthy, and the boy behind him turned to look at the one behind him, and so on.

"Don't look at someone else," sharply commanded the teacher. "I am speaking to you."

This attitude toward guilt has been common among us, particularly among those who live in the United States. Our history shows so many worthy deeds and so many responses to the cries of the hungry and oppressed that we have come to feel that we are the "good guys" and that the "bad guys" are in other countries. Personally, also, this inability to accept guilt has affected us as "Christians" and law-abiding citizens. When a bad deed is brought to light, our temptation has been to turn around to see who is the culprit. But since the end of World War II in 1945, this smugness has been changing to a more realistic appraisal of what we are and what we do. This change in attitude colors our devotional life.

Guilt accepted

As a sad matter of fact, but as an encouraging matter of fact also, a sense of guilt lies heavily upon our world. All joy of the common life is somewhat tempered by a guilt feeling. As we look for the reason for this acceptance of guilt, we think that we find among professing Christians an increasing awareness of the social implications of the teachings of the Bible. Among non-Christians some standard valid to them is beginning to show up their shortcomings in relation to other men and women. In the United States the conflict in Vietnam has brought soul-searchings as no other military involvement of our country has done before. Also, the present generation cannot rest easily with the knowledge of how white men have dealt with black men. Community and family problems add to the pang of guilt among us.

No doubt this new sensitivity to personal, racial, and national sins is a positive good. However, if this feeling of guilt becomes maudlin and unreasoning, it leads to emotional upsets and diminished ability to crusade for righteousness. In this chapter, our study of the message of the Bible and the Spirit concerning sin could lead us to a wholesome harnessing of our newfound truth that each of us is inextricably bound up in the human bundle of life; we must accept what the poet John Donne said when he heard the church bell tolling to announce the death of someone: "And therefore never send to know for whom the bell tolls; It tolls for thee."

Sins of yesterday

As we turn to Scripture for its teachings on sin and guilt, we find of course that the Bible cites instances of the sins of yesterday committed by the people of yesterday. These are the perennial sins, the typical sins that occur in any age or place. Mankind has not changed basically since the days the Bible was written.

For instance, in Second Samuel we read of the double sin of David. He was guilty of adultery and then of murder. Or the triple sin, we might say, because he, in common with the rebuked schoolboy, looked over his shoulder to find the sinner when the prophet Nathan told him of a man who had wronged his brother. Like the school teacher, Nathan was obliged to be abrupt and say to David, "You are the man."

Adultery and murder are still with us, although there is a tremendous effort to explain them away. In the new studies of situational and contextual ethics, those and other sins are examined in light of particular situations and in relation to other events. However, in the Bible we find an absoluteness of the word that these sins are sins no matter where or how they are committed.

The writer of Psalm 51 sums up his faults in the blanket term "transgressions." These transgressions may be found detailed as we read the Bible and follow the men and women whose lives are portrayed. In the Ten Commandments (Exodus 20) we find the sins of yesterday which are the sins of today: in addition to murder and adultery, included are theft, slander, coveting, and idolatry. None of these sins have been repealed. All are subjects of guilt.

Sins of today

In our day there is the temptation to adopt a category that sets us apart from the sinners of the past: Modern Man. Our society is so complex and vast that King David would think himself to be in a dream world of horrible proportions should he come among us. Our tools, our weapons, our businesses, our pleasures, our knowledge — yes, particularly our knowledge — are beyond the comprehension of a David. All of this, we think, puts our guilt in a setting different from that of David's.

For one thing, our guilt must be of a keener and more poignant type since we have learned the far-reaching effect of words and deeds. Our communications media are capable of seizing upon what we do or say and broadcasting our behavior to millions, and these millions may be made better or worse because of what we have done or said.

Further, we now know something of the enduring effects of sin. Formerly, a husband and father might be a drunkard and we limited the results of his sin to himself, to the visible bruises he might inflict on his wife or companions, to the hunger or other wants that might be the fate of his family. Now we speak of "trauma," the emotional or psychological wound given to a child which may condition that child's entire life. If a man or woman used drugs or smoked to excess, we limted the sin to the injury that he or she was doing to himself or herself. But now we know that the use of narcotics may result in abnormalities in the next generation.

Another point is that despite our being crowded together in endless cities we experience a remoteness from one another that David did not know, and this is seen especially in our sins. When David killed a man in warfare, he knew what he was doing. The combat was face-to-face. David knew whether or not he had done wrong and to whom. Now we elect representatives to Congress; these representatives (without asking our opinion) vote for a war or "police action"; they vote to tax us for defense; our money buys bombs; these bombs are dropped on a place such as Hiroshima; not even the bomber pilots see the people the bombs kill, much less do the representatives we have elected. Still less do we know whom we have hurt!

But despite what we think are differences between our moral and ethical responsibilities and those of the men of David's day, we must admit that every sinner has a basic kinship with every other sinner from the time of Cain. Every sinner has a gnawing need to resolve his guilt. Having done what he ought not to have done, having brought misery or death to others, what does the sinner do to "make it right"?

Confession

As our devotional life becomes deeper, we shall see more

clearly the urgency of confession. Even in medicine confession is required before healing can take place. The doctor wants to know: what have you been eating or drinking; what has been your sexual life; what are your working and sleeping schedules? Unless the patient is honest, the doctor will not know what to do about the ailment since he cannot know what induced it. In the fields of psychiatry and psychology, confession is even more a part of therapy. But our immediate concern over confession is the confession we make to God.

Confession is taught in the Bible in many places and is found in the "Starting Points" passage from First John. The prime purpose of confession is to prepare the heart for forgiveness. There can be no release from guilt until a sinner knows and will admit that he is a sinner. Many alcoholics go from bad to worse because they will not admit that they have a problem. The Alcoholics Anonymous group will not try to help a person unless he or she is ready to confess to alcoholism and the desire to be free of it. Confession is an acknowledgment to God of a sin committed, of a weakness that enslaves, of unworthy thoughts, of self-centeredness.

Forgiveness

Except in the rare case of exhibitionism where a sinner loves to boast of how bad he is, confession brings immediate results. In the first place, the wrongdoer knows his situation; all is out in the open. In *Great Expectations,* Charles Dickens relates the story of a young man who found himself in debt. He knew that he owed a number of people and firms. When one creditor brought pressure, he paid him something. But one day he tired of this vagueness. He bought a little account book, searched his records and his memory, and made a page for each debt. He put down the name of the creditor and the amount due. He said this took a great load from his mind just to know where he stood. Confession does this for us; we no longer reason away wrong deeds or blame others; honestly and frankly we know our condition.

Following this certainty of mind, we begin to sense that our relationship to God has changed: "If we confess our sins, he is faithful and just, and will forgive our sins and cleanse us from all unrighteousness" (1 John 1:9).

This forgiveness is more than a simple remission of penalty; indeed sin always exacts some penalty even though God has forgiven it. However, forgiveness removes the eternal penalty and restores the lost sheep to the fold and the lost son to the household. The story of what we call "The Prodigal Son" in Luke 15 is a good example. In exchange for the son's confession of his sin and his prayer for restoration, the father gladly forgave what his son had done, cleansed him, and gave him clean clothing and his old room in the house. But even the father could not give back to that young man the lost days and nights wasted in the far country nor the treasure and health that he had expended. The murderer can and may be forgiven after confession and repentance, but his victim cannot be brought back to life.

The restored person

What about us, then, after we have confessed and have felt God's forgiveness? What is our course of action and our outlook for tomorrow?

Surely, the restored person will have a better sense of identity with other sinners, both the unconfessed and the forgiven. If we enter into a state of restoration, we will no longer be prone to condemn everyone whom we know to be doing wrong or who is brought into court. If we are white, for instance, we will not pounce upon the horrible acts of blacks as if blacks are natural sinners; if we are black, we will not blame the whites for everything that has gone wrong for 450 years. Having come to a knowledge of our own sin, we shall be slow to act self-righteously when the sin of another seemingly is exposed.

Another characteristic of the truly restored person is his desire to make whatever restitution can be made. If we have done the obvious, such as extorting or stealing money (as was true of Zacchaeus [Luke 19]), we shall want to repay what we have taken. If our sin is less in the realm of the tangible, we shall find joy in giving ourselves and our time and substance in the field where we think our sin has been the worst. The sin of pride can be repaid by seeking out humble tasks in humble places for the relief of humble people. Some who have been drug addicts now work among the youth who are "on" drugs. Always we shall want to set up warnings or erect spiritual lighthouses to help others avoid what we have done or thought. In exchange for God's forgiveness, the writer of Psalm 51 promises to "teach transgressors thy ways" (verse 13) and speak to others of God's forgiveness, "my mouth shall show forth thy praise" (verse 15).

PRAYER PATTERN: O God, to whom all hearts are open and from whom no secrets are hid, accept my acknowledgment of my sins of commission and omission, especially the sin of not doing for my oppressed brothers what I ought to have done. Amen.

9
With God in Life's Depths

Starting Points: 1 John 4:13-19; Ephesians 3:14-21.

"Who is going to be with me when I am by myself?" asked a little boy whose mother was putting him to bed. That little boy voiced a question which haunts every one of us. Oh, we can usually find someone to talk to and walk with, but our inner person can still feel a sense of aloneness. Even if we resorted to going to Times Square in New York City which, of all places in the world, is noted for its throngs of people, we could be assailed by a depressing loneliness. Something within us cries out for the only companion who can come through the self-barriers that no human can breach; and that companion is God.

The alone part of us

If we ask why we are so made that there is always a part of us that cannot be shared even with our nearest and dearest, we may come to a mystery. The mystery seems to be that God has created each of us as a unique being. No one of us can be matched by any other person in the world or in history. We may find amazingly similar physical likenesses, but when we talk to that one who seems so much our twin, we find that we are poles apart in our selfhood.

Realizing this uniqueness may answer our questions about

our inability to "get through" to others, especially the young among us. The truth is that no one can get through completely to anyone, despite the new emphasis on communication which is with us now.

Should this knowledge of a reserved section in the individual cause us despair? Or, on the contrary, should it be of comfort to us? Both results may be found — despair because we reach out to others and feel them reaching out to us without success, and comfort when we remember that we have an inner core of being that is unassailable by any outside force. But the best result of discovering our aloneness is that we are driven to seek the only one who can come behind our walls and be our intimate friend.

The possible companion

In his unutterable glory, majesty, and power, God is pleased to make himself available to each one of us as soon as we discover that not all the millions of people who live in the world with us can take away our basic loneliness. Two familiar verses in the Bible assure us that God is our possible companion: "Behold, I stand at the door and knock; if any one hears my voice and opens the door, I will come in to him and eat with him, and he with me" (Revelation 3:20) and "I will not leave you desolate; I will come to you" (John 14:18).

As our creator, God knows what we are and understands us. To others we may be strange and unfathomable, but to God we are open and familiar. The part of us that cries for the divine companion is that part that is made in the "image of God" as we read in Genesis. With all reverence, we may say that we are akin to him. When there is a close relationship between God and us, we sense that there is something within us that God finds companionable and our worth is in terms of divine acceptance.

Divine-human relationship

When we come to grips with the need for a relationship

with God, we may be tempted to think that this is one experience that is added to all of the human experiences of relationship. If we yield to this temptation, we shall have nothing but a casual or superficial relationship with God, such as that which we have with some friends whom we remember only at Christmas. This relationship is that which brings us out to church on Easter and when we have need of a family baptism or wedding. This casual type of relationship we hope to overcome as, in this chapter, we look at the possibilities for deepening our fellowship with God.

The deeper the fellowship, the more we shall be convinced that a relationship with God is not on a level with other relationships but is that which colors and makes vital those other relationships. How then shall we go from the casual and intermittent to the deep and continual companionship with God? As usual, the Bible is a good "how-to" book in this respect.

The passage from First John shows us an entrance into a strong and fast relationship. The first requirement is to believe that Jesus is the Son of God. This is essential since our knowledge of God is based on what Jesus taught and demonstrated about him — "He who has seen me has seen the Father" (John 14:9). If we stay in the path of life followed by Christ, we can be sure that we are "abiding" with God.

Another suggestion from First John is that God's hand is outstretched to catch us as we struggle into his presence: "He first loved us" (1 John 4:19). We go up the path of love that has been paved by God for our ready footing. This path runs right through the midst of our fellowmen and is not a secret trail off the beaten track.

Strengthening the bonds

This relationship with God has been thought of by men as precarious and reversible. A generation or two ago the term "backslider" was used in churches to describe one who had "been saved" but who had lost his grip on God's hand and had fallen back into his old life of sin. Happily, provision was made for restoring these backsliders by a new experience of salvation at a revival or evangelistic meeting. Whatever we may think of this doctrine, we know that our first hold upon God can be tenuous and needs strengthening by daily experience in the devotional life. The selection from Ephesians is a good guide to this process of making the bond of our companionship with God strong.

We find that our "inner man" may be strengthened by the Spirit. We know that the outer man or woman may be strengthened by physical exercise and health programs, but the inner man is not changed by these disciplines; the inner man can be strengthened only by the exercise of fellowship in the Spirit. This truth holds encouragement for all of us since it matters not what physical handicaps we may have; a veritable Hercules is no better in this regard than a cripple bound to a wheelchair. In fact, that handicapped person may be stronger in the inner man than the Mr. or Miss America. It will depend upon the presence of the Spirit.

Next we find that our faith is a fortifier of the fellowship. Christ will dwell in us through faith. Many years ago a man named Coué came to the United States and offered a slogan: "Every day, in every way, I am getting better and better." He insisted that anyone who would base his life on this philosophy would soon be well, strong, and prosperous. The basic idea was a sort of self-hypnotism, the planting of an idea deep down in the self that eventually would bear good fruit. We find a better slogan for ourselves and one that can work toward a stronger faith: "I believe; help my unbelief!" (Mark 9:24). Sturdily voicing our belief will bring help from the Lord.

A third point from Ephesians is that we must be rooted and grounded in love. Just as a plant shows by its growth the richness or barrenness of the soil in which its roots are situated, so does the person show the kind of spiritual soil in which he is rooted. Love is our soil, our ground from which we draw the nourishment for our God-man companionship. Despite the ethical, moral, and religious pollution in the world, there is a deep layer of love among men that cannot be contaminated or eroded. It is in this layer of love that the companion of God must find his place and sink his roots down so deeply that no circumstance can persuade him to let go.

This rooting and grounding in love will bring us into a knowledge of the changeless love of God, and we shall be filled with the fullness of the Lord. If we have been scared at the slenderness of our tie with God at the beginning, we may remember how it is with a person who has been without food or water for a time. When that person is rescued, he must not be told, "Here is a good steak dinner, and here is a pitcher of ice water; help yourself!" No, he must be given water and food sparingly until he is back to normal. Life's adventures and heartbreaks can estrange us from God until we may need to take in his fullness little by little. Our relationship is secure when we are able to accept all of God that he is waiting to give us, and when we make ourselves willing to experience all that he can be to us. This process is one of the richest possible in the devotional life.

Deeper and deeper

At this point the readers may ask, "What does the author mean by 'deeper and deeper'? We are so deep now that we are lost; we are a practical people and we live among practical people. We need something we can lay hold upon!" Fair enough. But we must admit that we are complex persons and that the intangible self is greater than the "five-senses" self. Even so, there are illustrations to help.

Take love, for instance. No matter how old or how young we are at this moment, which of us has not, at one time at least, "fallen in love"? Do we remember that magic moment when we knew that our feeling for some other person flooded our being and that the whole world was changed? Were we able then, or are we able now, to outline that feeling in A-B-C fashion? We must accept that our relationship with God is in this same realm of love and we cannot dissect it, but we can know when it is there. This companion feeling is no more nor less mysterious than the giving of ourselves in love to another. And this new relationship with God will continue to prove itself in a new life pattern and an inner peace.

The life work of an astronomer is another illustration that is "down-to-earth." The astronomer gives his days and many of his nights, year after year, to the measuring, listing, classifying, and observing of stars. He will think his life work a success if he discovers a new star or one small new law governing the movements of what he sees in the skies. Nothing is achieved unless he gives of himself hour after hour. So it is with us if we desire to enter into the depths of life with God. This cannot be done by giving to the matter one fraction of the time we spend watching television. God is the creator of what the astronomer is willing to give his life to study; we shall never grasp God's greatness, but we can approach that greatness until we are expanded out of our narrowness and earth-bound aspirations.

Now we look again at that path of love which we saw winding around through the "crowded ways of life." If we are on the love path to God, we shall find our way only by exhibiting that love to our fellowman. In Matthew 25:31-46, which some call the "Judgment Scene," we see lined up the strangers, the hungry, thirsty, naked, sick, and imprisoned people who need God's love given through *us*. It will do us no good to "symbolize" or "spiritualize" these haunting figures; their need is desperate and real.

In our day, with all the technological advances, there are millions who never have enough to eat; there are arid places in the world where water is scarce; there are persons in minority groups whom we have treated as strangers in our homes, churches, and businesses; there is inadequate medical care for countless people; there are inhuman conditions in our prisons; many millions need the Good News.

If we are earnest in our desire to deepen our relationship with God, we must be out on the road of God's love where we find the "least of his brethren." We wanted the tangible, something to lay hold upon, and here it is! If we want to be where God is and "abide" with him, if we want to be rid of that loneliness within, we shall be out on the road of love that goes to the cross.

For our reward in our devotional life, we shall find that at the deeper levels of fellowship with God there are surprising riches of grace and peace and joy.

PRAYER PATTERN: O Divine Companion, I know I lack something today. There is an ache within, a reaching out for you. Come into my heart! Amen.

10

Sharing Worship Experience

Starting Points: Psalm 122; 1 Corinthians 11:23-28; Hebrews 10:23-25.

A man who had inherited several million dollars, according to a newspaper story of several years ago, was so happy with his new wealth that he scattered money around him as he walked along the street. He advertised that he would help people in need. He could not endure to be so well cared for without sharing his good fortune with others. Do we not share that feeling when we become aware that the Spirit is our guest and that God is our constant companion? How can we withdraw secretly to enjoy our release from loneliness? How can we resist following the example of the apostles Peter and John who answered the authorities who had commanded them to keep still: "We cannot but speak of what we have seen and heard" (Acts 4:20)? A close relationship to God results in this kind of exuberance.

Worship is private

However, despite our overwhelming desire to make public what has come to us, we shall find that just as our devotional experience of finding God as companion is private so our worship will always be a private thing. In the last analysis, we cannot worship for others nor can they worship for us. Deep worship experiences are personal and individual.

But we help each other

This private aspect of worship does not mean, however, that we may not engage in worship at the same time and in the same place with others. Indeed, the Bible directs that we shall gather ourselves together at certain seasons and on set days for the purpose of joint worship. The Spirit gives a plus to our lives when two or three or more come together to praise God. The result is something like the sound of a great organ in a church or cathedral. The music comes from compressed air being released through many pipes of various sizes. Each pipe has its own tone and sweetness, and each helps the other pipes produce one grand melody. Each of us is familiar with his own gift of worship, but there is a lift to all when we help each other in corporate worship of the Lord. We remember, though, that each pipe is separate and that there is no fusing into one large pipe. So we find, again, that each of us must worship singly even though there is an added blessing as we join each other in the congregational praise.

Mutual experiences

We look now at some of the mutual experiences of congregational or group worship. In Psalm 122 we follow the trip of a pilgrim as he goes up to Jerusalem to worship with others. He has been invited to go and he has invited others to go. On the way all of the pilgrims sing praises to God and pause at times for prayers. We, too, have been invited to start off for the heavenly Jerusalem and we plead with others to join in the procession; at times we engage in joint worship, reminding one another that there is a goal ahead in the kingdom of God.

The early pilgrims to Jerusalem found that worship was a unifying force. They had one purpose which they were expressing by their direction and by their devotions. In our experience, the church has become the symbol of unity for all who are on the journey toward God. What we call "membership in the church" becomes to us a pledge of unity. As the psalmist found, participants in group worship seek the "peace" and "good" of one another. An hour or more a week spent together in worship has mighty possibilities for us, for others, for the nation, and for the world.

Another mutual experience is mentioned in the passage from First Corinthians, the Lord's Supper. The observance of the Lord's Supper has become a regular part of congregational worship. Even though each one partakes of the bread and wine symbols individually, rarely is this done privately. Perhaps Christ had this in mind when he served his followers at the Passover and instituted this part of worship as a reason for believers to come together regularly.

We can find the meaning of the Lord's Supper in the term "Eucharist" which is often used as a name for the Communion. Eucharist comes from a Greek word meaning "thanksgiving." The Lord's Supper, then, is not a time of hopeless mourning over the death of Jesus, but an occasion of thanksgiving that he did die for the whole world. Even though we remember the shed blood and nail-pierced hands and feet, we have in the back of our minds the glad knowledge that he is alive forevermore. And this mutual experience at the table brings forth in us a desire to evaluate our motives; why are we together at the table thinking solemn thoughts? We test ourselves for genuineness as gold is tested, and we sense that our fellow worshipers are examining themselves also.

So far we have taken for granted that all who have found God as companion do come together for mutual worship experiences and to help one another. But church attendance statistics do not bear this out. Taken from records at random, one New England church of 1100 members registered 55 at a morning service in August, 1971. An English church of 1500 members reports an average morning congregation of 25! Of course, there are better situations but the trend around the world is not favorable. In the verses from Hebrews we find that this condition existed in the early church as well. The writer reminds his readers that they need to come together to encourage one another, especially in view of the fact that each passing hour brings nearer the "day" of the last times.

Each adds his share

In the illustration of the organ pipes we saw how each one may and must add his share to the worship experience. In Hebrews we have noted that encouragement is needed. In the group called "Alcoholics Anonymous," which we mentioned earlier, men and women with the problem of alcoholism come together regularly to encourage one another in their hard battle against the strong desire for liquor. They relate to one another their triumphs and their miserable times and assure one another that victory is possible and worthwhile. They go from the meeting with new strength to win new victories. In a way, a church congregation is a group of redeemed sinners who are still obliged to fight the old temptations day by day. Each one may relate God's dealings with him and encourage others to go on in the way of purposeful and triumphant Christian living.

As each worshiper encourages another, he may add his share to the ritual of the service. Singing is better for the addition of the voices of all. Solos have their merit, but what can equal part-singing where deep voices and high voices, where altos, basses, tenors, and sopranos join in a magnificent harmony? Singing together, we express to God the deep emotions of our heart: joy, mourning, love, longing, belligerence against evil and wrong, family ties, and thanksgiving.

All may join in formal prayer. Even though one may "lead," each one engages in his own moment of prayer and the joint prayers go out to God in a great petition for the peace and welfare of all mankind. As we pray together, we shall find that our prayers are more likely to rise above personal concern and embrace the wider fellowship than when we kneel in private.

We are challenged, also, by periods of readings and responses in which all may participate. In teaching techniques, it is generally conceded that learning depends upon the amount of personal participation. This is true in worship as well. Our devotional level is raised by unison response to some great truth that has been read from the lesson.

Let us not omit the joint sacrifice of giving. We say sacrifice because the offering is the nearest thing we have to the ancient sacrifice of goods in kind. No longer do we bring the produce of our garden or an animal from our barn, or an article of wood from the shop, or a loaf of bread from the oven; we change these things into money and give that as our sacrifice. The sum of what we all bring can accomplish much that would be impossible for one person to do.

When we come to a sermon, we may think that we are not adding to that at all. The preacher has done the work of preparing and is now doing the work of delivering. But let us look at what the sermon is intended to be. From early times the sermon has been the proclamation of the Good News. As we sit and listen, we add to the sermon by our inner assent to the truth. Any preacher will admit that the success of his sermon depends largely on the feeling of attention that comes up to him from the audience. How can a servant of God preach the Good News when the people are drowsy, fidgety, whispering, or otherwise indicating that they will be glad when the service comes to an end? If the gospel is to be preached to others, we must add our share to the preaching by being in attendance and by witnessing to the truth through our alertness in listening and in thinking about the expounded Word.

In addition to the parts of the worship ritual mentioned is the reading of the Scripture. Protestants, particularly, have made the Bible central in worship. They know that from it stem the hymns, prayers, readings, and sermons. No service is complete without the reading of some portion of the Bible. Here again, even a listener adds his share to the success of the reading by attention and by fixing anew the familiar words that are being brought to congregational notice. At each reading we may pledge once more to make the word a "lamp to our feet and a light to our path." (See Psalm 119:105.)

Blazing new trails

The customary course of worshiping as a group or congregation comes under criticism from time to time. Our young people, particularly, wonder why the old, old forms need to be continued generation after generation. The Roman Catholic church as a church is raising the same question on a worldwide scale. Attempts are being made to blaze new trails that will take worshipers in better ways to "Jerusalem." A fresh wind of change blows among us in our time.

In one experiment in worship the congregation is seated facing one another in a round sort of room. Spontaneity of response after a sermon is encouraged. The preacher does not end unquestioned, but the worshipers are encouraged to agree or disagree with his dissertation and to add any insight that has come to them during the preaching. In fact, some sermons are given in dialogue or panel fashion. New hymns and new arrangements for old hymns and anthems are being written. The organ is sometimes omitted in favor of stringed or brass instruments. Litanies speaking to and of the world are being introduced. All of this can be good if we maintain our reverence and our sense of the holy presence of God. The test of any worship pattern is whether or not it is effective in sending the worshipers back into the world with greater hope, faith, and courage and with a keener desire to serve their brothers and sisters.

PRAYER PATTERN: Father God, even in the great congregation I know that I must touch you for myself, but I pray that I may have something to add to the joint worship of your people. I pray that I may be humble enough to see and seize the excellency of anything shared by another. Amen.

11

High Moments in the Family

Starting Points: Deuteronomy 6:1-9; Psalm 78:1-8; 2 Timothy 1:3-7.

Have we put this chapter in the wrong place? We started with the devotional life of the individual; then we took the individual into the company of a congregation. But now we go back to a smaller group, the family. Should not this progression have been from one to a family and then to the larger gathering? The fact is that the guiding factor is not in numbers but in difficulty of performance. The easiest sort of devotional life is that carried on in private as we go apart or draw ourselves away from the rush of life. Sharing this devotional grace with many others is harder, but participating in a genuine devotional life before and with our family is hardest of all.

The difficulty lies in being under the judgment of those with whom we live. A father is watched most carefully by wife and children, a wife by husband and children, children by both parents; and we might go on to aunts, uncles, and grandparents. Those with whom we live see us at our worst and convincing them that we are without hypocrisy and sham when we engage in family worship is not easy. But participating in family worship is possible and is essential to a total devotional experience. Do we see that this chapter is in the right order?

What is a family?

"Am I a family?" asked an unmarried woman who lived alone. A discussion of helps for family worship had been held in a group meeting. The woman's question set off a lively interchange of opinions. It was decided that on the rolls of a church this woman's household would be considered a family unit, and for census and other legal purposes she might be listed under the family category. But she could not be a family at worship since that involves sharing. A suggestion was that she might find other single people nearby and ask them if for the purpose of regular or occasional devotions they would not like to gather as a family, meeting in one of the homes.

Stirctly speaking, a family must have at least two persons, and our general concept is beyond that, one or two parents living with children.

The great commandment

At the heart of the high moments of family devotions is the great commandment. To find out which is the great commandment, we may review the question of a scribe who came to Jesus and asked that very thing. When we find that at the time of Jesus the rabbis listed 613 binding commandments that could be found in the Law, we can see that Jesus had a wide choice for choosing *the* commandment (Mark 12:28-34). But he did not hesitate; he quoted from the passage in Deuteronomy that we are using as a guide: "Hear, O Israel: The Lord our God, the Lord is one; and you shall love the Lord your God with all your heart, and with all your soul, and with all your mind, and with all your strength" (Mark 12:29-30). This commandment was known to the Israelites as the *Shema,* the Hebrew for "hear," which is the first word of the commandment. The *Shema* was used to open synagogue services and was to be repeated twice a day by every faithful Jew.

For our present attention, however, the important part of

the selection from Deuteronomy is the injunction that all parents are to teach this "great commandment" to their children. Undoubtedly the children would hear it in the synagogue or from a rabbi, but that did not excuse the parents from their responsibility. They were not to turn over the religious instruction of their children to others as we often do when we "send" our boys and girls to church school. The teaching of this commandment in homes may be the earliest example of family worship, or one of the earliest. A family of our day could do no better than start out the devotional period with this commandment and a discussion of it.

Importance of family worship

Thinking again of the Jewish family, we realize that likely the Jewish family was more isolated from others than our families are and, therefore, depended upon a self-sufficient program of religious instruction and worship. In a sense, however, a family in our day is isolated within a pluralistic community and needs the strength of family solidarity in seeking God just as much as or more than the rural group of Israelites.

In Psalm 78 we are again reminded of the importance of family worship. One is to keep unbroken the continuity of teaching God's word and meditating upon it. If our children are not taught as we were, how shall they teach their children? Despite the laxness and failure of many families to preserve the pattern of family devotions, enough families have been faithful to the point of saving for us the *Shema* and all that stems from it. Two things growing out of the study of this commandment are hope in God and the keeping of his laws.

This psalm gives us an unexpected slant for family worship. Perhaps we had thought that the continuity of worship would result in molding our children in our pattern. But the psalmist says our children are to be taught that "they should not be like their fathers" (verse 8) ! That this teaching has been fruitful is proved by observing how our young people are turning from money for money's sake, from war, and from claiming privilege because of race or circumstance.

In 2 Timothy 1:5, Paul reminds Timothy that through the faith of his mother and grandmother he was brought to faith in God. Here is another phase of the importance of family worship; boys and girls who will be the men and women of tomorrow must be given an opportunity to examine the faith of their fathers and to check that faith by its results in the lives and work of the older generation. If there are no preachers, teachers of religion, or missionaries in the days ahead, the family will be as much to blame as the church. When the author, as a young man, came to his first parish in Philadelphia, he looked up the records and found his church had not sent forth a young person to study for the pastoral ministry for *fifty years!* We might ask, what had the parents and grandparents been teaching their children during that time?

Family worship can play an important part in solving "the generation gap." Two or three generations can be brought closer together by sharing in a humble effort to find God's will for each life in these turbulent days. When children hear the father and mother expressing their faith and see how their standard of behavior grows out of that faith, they have a better understanding of the discipline of the home. The parents' dos and don'ts seem less arbitrary when they appear as part of the pattern of accepted Christian standards.

Overcoming obstacles

Many family members admit the beauty and helpfulness of family sessions of worship and study, but they bemoan the fact that "it is just impossible" for them. Time seems to be the chief enemy of family worship in this day. Every year people become more and more involved in things outside the home, and many of the involvements are worthy.

How can all members of a family stop for a brief period together? One way of solving this problem is to have a family conference and agree on an arbitrary period or periods (daily or weekly) for the worship and to keep faith with these determined times no matter who may be absent. Thus the absent ones, such as the father on a business trip or a young person away in college or military service, could feel that the family was gathered at that time and prayers were being offered.

Another obstacle lies in the diffidence of parents. Many say they feel awkward or ill at ease in leading worship and speaking of their deepest convictions before their children. Sometimes this is the result of the parents' keen sense of their own imperfections. They dread to act "pious" when they know that their children are well aware of their shortcomings and that they note how clumsy the parents may be in leading in prayer and reading aloud. Unhappily, if this lack of confidence is permitted to cancel any hopes for family worship, the children could grow up with the same diffidence when they have homes of their own. A solution may be found by going ahead with the family worship no matter how amateurish the devotions may be; the longer there is practice in this, the less timidity and clumsiness there will be. Confidence and skill will come in time, and the children likely will admire the courage of a parent who does what comes hard for him or her.

Still another reason why some families omit group worship is in the fear that sincerity cannot be achieved. There is a great aversion among us, particularly among younger people, toward phoniness. This can be a real threat to the value of the worship. If the routine is mere routine, if the worship is rushed, or if there is an irritability about "getting it over with," much is lost. Or if children sense that parents are urging the devotional period because they have read that it is a good influence on children, it will no doubt be ineffective. Genuineness is possible if the period set aside for the family to come together is treated as though it is at

81

least as important as a meal or a favorite TV show; and if the parents indicate that they rely upon this opportunity to gain strength for *their* needs, there should be no backlash.

Some "how to's"

Naturalness is the watchword for family worship. If in a family the attitude can be cultivated that persons are created to require food, drink, sleep, recreation, love, work, and worship and that life is sadly incomplete if one or more of these needs are lacking, then worship can become a natural part of the day's expectations and activities.

One of the simplest acts of family worship is thanksgiving or "grace" said before or after meals. Varying these can add knowledge and richness to the occasion. Taking turns in saying the grace gives responsibility to all members of the family and could call for research to find fresh and meaningful expressions of gratitude. Holding hands around the table may soften some momentary bitterness that exists.

Prayers at night and/or morning are possible and bring a blessing to the home.

Readings from the Bible sometime during the week, shared by each person old enough to take his turn, will engrave some eternal words in the hearts and minds of all. If the selections coincide with the church school lesson for the coming Sunday, so much the better. Each member of the family might bring his own Bible to the reading and follow the selection.

If there is a piano or organ in the home, impromptu hymn sings add zest to the worship and help provide a congenial atmosphere.

The new approaches to worship mentioned earlier could spur the family on to some creativity of its own to get away from the tried-and-true methods. Whoever has a musical instrument, no matter what it is, could utilize it for a change of pace. Young people might bring back some innovations after attending youth groups or retreats.

A helpful or disturbing article from a newspaper or magazine could be introduced by any member of the family for discussion as to how the family might understand the situation or be of help.

Devotional booklets with daily portions including a selected Scripture passage, a meditation, and a prayer likely can be found in your church. While the regular use of these without anything else in the worship period may bring too much routine to the period and stifle ambition for independent methods, such booklets can be of service as a beginning and as thought starters.

PRAYER PATTERN: O Lord of hearth and home as well as of sanctuary and marketplace, give a vision to all who earnestly desire to have family devotions in spirit and in truth. Amen.

12

Devotion and Service

Starting Points: Matthew 17:1-20; John 15:1-11.

An athlete goes into intensive training. He submits to a carefully selected diet that will strengthen him and keep him lean. He jogs and runs mile after mile each day. He avoids debilitating pleasures and goes to bed early. He is out in the fresh air away from cities. He practices some skill, such as running, boxing, or throwing or hitting a ball. To what purpose is all this discipline and energetic "getting into shape"? Is it merely that the athlete may go back among his friends and enjoy his fine glow of health and amuse himself with the skills he has learned? Of course not! The athlete goes into training rigorously to prepare for a track meet, a boxing match, a football or baseball season. He has made himself ready for some event that will challenge the best he has to give.

We may think of this plan of the athlete as similar to our plan of training in our devotional life. We have been searching out the ways toward spiritual strength; we have looked at Bible study, prayer, faith, praise, and confession. But why are we engaging in these devotional exercises? Do we do them because we want to go through life happy in the fine glow of our assurance of God's presence and guidance? In the words of an old song, perhaps we plan to sing —

I'll sit and sing myself away
To everlasting bliss.

As with the athlete, we are bound to say, "Of course not!" The preparation in the devotional life is for the high purpose of serving and witnessing. In this chapter we are to look at service.

Why good things come

We may start with a question: Can we conceive of God's giving to some of his children surpluses of spiritual, mental, and physical goods and possessions while other of his children are lacking in these blessings? We know that surpluses do come to us from time to time. Why do these good things come?

A family that came to the notice of the author had an adequate regular income that kept the members from need. Occasionally small checks would come in unexpectedly as a result of past services rendered by the father. When such a check came, the family would inquire: "What is this money for?" Almost invariably, the family related, a letter from someone in need, a plea from some worthy cause, or a family emergency would follow hard upon the heels of the check's arrival. God had sent the money; he sent also the knowledge of where it could be put to the best use. This illustration may seem more dramatic than that which happens to us ordinarily, but it is typical of the law of surpluses sent from God.

Indeed, the passage from Matthew, the story of what happened on the Mount of Transfiguration, expresses the same thing. Peter, James, and John were so happy at having been selected by Jesus as his companions for the trip up the mountain and were so overwhelmed with joy at being permitted to see Moses and Elijah that they had but one desire, let this go on forever. Jesus had to point out to them that they had not come to the heights for selfish enjoyment. He took them down to the foot of the mountain where they found the illness and suffering and varied needs of mankind.

The moments of exultation had been a preparation for extensive service.

In John 15 we are warned of the consequences of keeping God's blessing to ourselves. A believer is spoken of as a branch that has the great honor of being attached to Christ, the vine. This attachment to the Lord insures care and nourishment, but the branch must bear fruit. For the first time, we see that there is a penalty for taking in the good things of God and failing to share them; the fruitless branch will be broken from the vine. Among the twelve disciples, Judas proved to be a fruitless branch and lost his fellowship with his Lord. If there is no service to God and man growing out of our devotional life, then it may become dull and unreal.

We are tempted at times to take the warm assurance of the church fellowship and of personal and corporate worship without accepting the obligation of putting the shoulder to the wheel of service.

Worship and service married

Too often, worship and service are viewed as having no real connection. As in school when we took one subject in one room and then moved to another room for a second subject the subjects seemed unrelated; so worship and service may appear unrelated. English I and Trigonometry do not seem to depend on one another; likewise, the mundane things of ministering to the bodily needs of the underprivileged do not seem to be related to the antiseptic and secluded acts of worship. Like it or not, however, there cannot be worship without service or service without worship. Worship may be thought of as a powerhouse or a recharging room from which we come to release God's energy and love into the sordid world of man's sins, poverty, disgrace, and violence.

At this point let us look at a temptation of our time. In their impatience, many advocate dispensing with the formal acts of worship and the mystic quiet times of life in favor of devoting all time and all life to involvement with the urgent needs of men, women, and children. To them service *is* worship. There is some truth in this, of course, but not the whole truth. Service can be the natural extension of worship, but service is not self-starting. Service in the last analysis needs a reservoir of power that comes of waiting in God's presence. We remember that after the death of Jesus the disciples obeyed his prior instructions to wait in Jerusalem until they received power by the Holy Spirit (Acts 1:1-11). Only after they had waited and had received the Holy Spirit did they begin their ministrations and healings.

Selective service

The ministrations and healings of the disciples were not carefully selected; whatever need presented itself became the prime issue of the moment. Contrasted to this is our tendency to select the kind of service we would like to render. In Philadelphia many years ago a man exercised this selectiveness. He found that he had been blessed with an overabundance of money. The church he attended needed a new building to carry on an essential work in the community. The man paid for a handsome and well-equipped structure and had his name put on the tower. This worked well as long as that neighborhood needed the church and the man's friends understood his good intentions. But there came a time when the church had outlived its usefulness in that locality; the man and his friends had died; the only thing left was a hard-and-fast gift agreement that provided that that man's name would always be on any church that his money provided. But in a new area of the city a church was needed and the money was offered to the new congregation with the limitation of the name. The new congregation, however, wanted to call its building "The Church of the Savior." The man's selectiveness of service thwarted a much needed new work. We shall find that if we carefully select what we will and will not do, our service eventually will come to bear our name rather than the name of the Lord, for his work is universal and constantly changing.

One good test of our service and our approach to it is to look honestly at the kind of relationship we have to the work to be done. When a church sent out a questionnaire asking each member what kind of service he was willing to perform, the answers were surprising. Many would serve as trustees, deacons, or chairmen of prominent committees, but few offered to help clean the building or to go out on a door-to-door canvass of the community. We might ask ourselves, "Will the work I choose depend on me so much that it will stop if I am voted out of office next year?" Do we make contributions at the proper time and in the proper amount to give us the maximum in tax deductions? Is the work we have in mind something that we feel sure God is putting before us to be done now? These questions provide another reason for starting out with worship; if we reach out to him, God will give us visions of what we should do.

Only as workmen ready to give ourselves to God for service in *his* harvest fields at any time and place can we experience the utmost of joy in the work. Sometimes as we sit in our pew on Sunday morning and listen to a sermon, do not we feel moved by an intensity of willingness that captures us? We long to be beyond the easy classification of do-gooders and to exhibit more than the world sees in professional humanitarians. If only we can work as though we were building a whole kingdom for God, we could add a service to our service.

Working together

We have seen how the man in Philadelphia built a church; he did not ask for help. But is there any place in God's plan for the lone wolf? In the first place, the branches must stay in the vine, which means that the worker is laboring with the Lord from the beginning. Then there are God's other workmen engaged in the task on an equal basis of importance with us. There was a time when Elijah thought he was the only workman God had left in the world, but God showed him how wrong he was (1 Kings 19:14-18). The fellowship of men, women, and young people who are joined in the Lord's work is like no other fellowship in all the world. That fellowship brings a great comfort because of the knowledge that shoulder to shoulder we are doing God's will and that everything does not depend on just one of us. That is one of the marvelous things about a congregation; generation after generation the church witnesses and serves in the world, and those who fall are replaced by others. When, according to tradition, Peter was crucified and Paul beheaded, they had no thought that God's work would come to an end with them.

The savor of service

Returning to the New Testament figure of the vine and the branches, we may carry the lesson a step further than we find in the few verses from John. If we in our world look at a vine — for example, a grape vine — we shall see that the fruit is borne on the branches. In the vine are the eternal principles of growth and through the vine flows the vital sap. Growing out of the vine and reaching farther into the surrounding world are the branches. By being privileged to bear the fruit, the branches demonstrate to the world the unseen richness that is in the vine. Thus, as people of an intimate relationship with God, we prove to men the life that we have in God by producing the fruit, the service.

For the grapes, men come to the vine, and the fruit is what they grasp. Except for the color and odor of the grapes and men's remembrance of former times when the grapes refreshed them, none would be drawn to the vine. This fact should indicate to us how serviceable we may be to Christ. We are commissioned to reach out into the world so that men will look to us thinking that we may supply their needs. If what men find in us is good, if our fruits are so satisfying that they want no better, we may be able to persuade them to be grafted onto the vine, even as we are. We cannot expect that others will desire God if they come and find what fruit we are bearing is harsh, selfish, and sour.

A final thought that may come to us from the two selections we have used as "Starting Points" is this: We, as Christians with a growing devotional life, have been put in the blessed position of temporary receivers and transmitters and not in the position of a Dead Sea into which freshness flows and stagnates because there is no adequate outlet.

PRAYER PATTERN: O Lord, our Lord, how excellent is your work! And how full you have filled me with things beyond my worth and my imagining! Show me where I am to bestow the surplus of strength, of love, of material goods that have come to me this day. Amen.

13

Joy to Spread Abroad

Starting Points: Acts 4:13-21; 8:26-40.

Before the days of the diesel engine and electric motors, steam engines were used to move our railroad trains. A steam-powered locomotive was an exciting thing to watch! When the fire had burned under the boiler long enough to build up a "head of steam," one of two things had to be done: a valve had to be opened to release the steam or the steam had to be directed into the piston chambers to make the locomotive roar along the track. We might think of the fire of our devotional life burning under our inner being until there is such an available amount of power in our lives that something must be done about it. The exultation may be released in public praise of God as we considered in chapter 10, or it may be put to work to carry us along the track of service as we reviewed in chapter 12. Now, as the final exploration of the devotional life, we shall try to enter into a third expression of the new life in God that pulses within us; this expression we call witnessing.

What is witnessing?

Public praise and service in the world are more easily understood than witnessing. To understand witnessing better, consider this simple illustration. In the lower grades of our schools, many teachers set aside a frequent period known as "Show and Tell." At that time the boys and girls are permitted to display before the class something that has come to them, such as a toy, a souvenir from a trip, a new article of clothing, or a book from the library, and they tell the class what it is, what it does, and what it means. When the authorities warned Peter and John not to speak or teach about Jesus, the disciples replied that they could not remain quiet, they must "show and tell" (Acts 4:20). This is witnessing.

We can learn much about witnessing from Peter and John. In the first place, witnessing is a response to compulsion. Witnessing is showing the wonderful things God has done for us and going among men wherever the driving power of our new life sends us. A seminary professor had compulsion in mind when he counseled his class: "Don't preach if you can help it!" As witnesses we shall find that we cannot help witnessing; if we can avoid it, then there is no compulsion of the Spirit.

As compulsion describes witnessing, so does boldness. Courage, forthrightness, and absolute assurance are the outward proofs of faith. In a church the pastor demonstrated boldness as he preached of sin and the judgment of God. After the service some of the officials remonstrated with him: he was preaching to decent people; did he need to be so positive on the subject of sin and its results? Then boldness left the man, and he said he must have been carried away and he was sorry! But it is just that being carried away that proves the authenticity of the Good News that the witness is sharing.

A third characteristic of witnessing is that one does not need to be a professional to be a witness. The early disciples were not trained as rabbis; they were not priests, prophets, or teachers of the law. This did not daunt them. Being what we call laymen did not hold them back from telling men about the Lord. They were like witnesses before a court of law. The witness will be heard despite his lack of academic degrees and expert qualification; the court wants to know what he *saw*.

This compulsion, boldness, and disregard of worldly training will impress men and women with the fact that the witness has "been with Jesus." Here is the great secret of effective witnessing. If our viewers and hearers can forget us and be caught up in what we are trying to show and tell, then results will come.

What happens?

If the engine we mentioned had built up the head of steam and the engineer opened a valve and no great white plume of steam arose from the stack, or if he engaged the gears and the wheels of the locomotive did not turn, what could be the trouble? The only explanation could be that the engineer had read the gauge wrong and there was no steam after all. When there is a "head of steam," something is going to happen! The same is true of our witnessing. If we really have had an experience of God and we show and tell, something is bound to happen, otherwise we must admit that we have just imagined our state of fervor.

When Peter and John witnessed, a man who was a cripple was healed. In our day when our doctors and psychologists are telling us that the greater portion of our physical and emotional ills stem from our mental attitudes, we should be impelled to tell men how God can and does heal minds. So often we draw back and advise the ill to go to psychiatrists and clinics, which are good and do what they can, but the power of God ought to be the first thing that we, as witnesses, offer. An expert in the health field has dared to say that a happy person of good habits has an excellent chance of avoiding *cancer*. He contends that fear, anxiety, pessimism, fretfulness, prejudice, and hate set us up for the onslaught of the deadly disease. These mental attitudes plus an indulged and undisciplined physical life lead us head-on toward cancer. If this man in his research has discovered something, then we, as witnesses, have something from

God that can change the attitudes mentioned above to faith, love, compassion, optimism, and joy and bring dedication to a temperate life. And this will help to bring healing.

What else happens? In the second passage from the Acts we go with Philip as he meets and witnesses to a eunuch. The witnessing results in the eunuch's understanding the Scripture and seeking to give himself to God in baptism. This should be the standard result of witnessing: Those who hear will earnestly desire to be part of the fellowship of believers. The true church grows because of witnessing and not by carefully prepared drives for new members. The three thousand who were added to the church when Peter preached on the day of Pentecost (Acts 2:41) were probably never put on an Inactive List of their congregation, and the eunuch to whom Philip witnessed probably did not have to be urged to come to meetings and give his share of money!

Witnessing inevitably crosses all racial and class lines. This brings greater vitality to the fellowship of believers. Some years ago a study was made of old New England families to show how many of the early names had disappeared. The chief reason given was that the aristocratic old families had intermarried for generations and sterility had set in. The researchers found that the men whose family names had survived had married young women of Italian, Irish, Polish, or other ethnic stocks. New vitality had come from the other nationalities. A newness came into religion when the apostles finally broke out of the little Jewish circle and went abroad to witness to the Gentiles.

Responsibility to witness

Perhaps if all men, women, boys, and girls around the world — at present about three billion of them — knew and followed the Lord, we would not need to witness. Oh, we could not help talking to one another about God's greatness and love; there would be no need, however, to proclaim the Good News. But we know from our personal contacts, from TV and radio, from magazines and newspapers that the world is far from the ideal state of being the kingdom of God. Without God in their hearts men are in racial strife, engaging in ghastly wars, permitting unparalleled luxury to exist alongside abject poverty, polluting the beautiful world that God has given them. Crime, despair, emotional breakdowns, and lax morality are expected aspects of today's world. The world needs God just as we need him. Our responsibility to "show and tell" is as great or greater than was that of the first disciples.

This responsibility is akin to that of a scientist or doctor who discovers a new medicine or method of treatment; ethically he may not keep the new thing to himself but must publish it for the free use of all.

The responsibility of witnessing begins with our witness by living. The life of a witness is his first and best witness. How can we try to heal the world unless we are treating men of all races as brothers, unless we are peacemakers, unless we have an active compassion for the needy?

Power for witnessing

As we have seen, the locomotive engineer could not do anything with his engine until the gauge indicated stored-up power ready for use. How can we get our power from our devotional life so that we may witness effectively?

The "Starting Point" passages must have convinced us that even the men who had walked with Jesus for three years, and who had seen him after the Resurrection, were not prepared or permitted to witness until the Spirit had come upon them. This is a hard thing for us to realize in our twentieth-century life. How can we tell whether or not the Spirit is with us? The old signs of speaking in tongues, of being visibly shaken by an outpouring of power, and of miracles seldom appear among us. We may find help in this puzzlement by remembering that Nicodemus also was puzzled. He could not understand what Jesus meant when he told him that he must be born again. Then Jesus told him that the Spirit is as unseen as the wind, coming and going quietly. (See John 3:5-9.)

The great test of a Spirit-filled life is found in what happens. If we are changed persons who are filled with love for all people because of an experience of nearness to God, and if that love expresses itself in complete commitment to the service of God and men, we have received the Spirit. If our witnessing brings results, the power of the Spirit is at work. Paul spoke of "signs and wonders" that followed from his witnessing (Romans 15:19) ; something always happened. Even if people did not accept as true what Paul was showing and telling them, there was still a power in that witnessing that caused them to respond. Their reaction often was violent and Paul was stoned and beaten. But the witness was affecting people. Stephen, also, had results when he witnessed even though he died; in fact his death was a "happening." If we witness by living and witness by telling and nothing happens, we need to go back to our quiet place and seek the power from God.

As we come to the end of our search for a deep devotional life, as we close our exploration into the possibilities that come from living in the presence of God, we should be well on our way to ever new and ever more wonderful experiences of the spirit. Each revelation of God's greatness and steadfast love will deposit with us something that can never be taken from us and about which our witness can never diminish. As Neil Armstrong and the others who have walked on the moon will never have that experience dimmed or canceled, and as they will always insist that they did walk on the moon, so we who are accepted into the holy presence of God will have a story to tell that no one may contradict.

PRAYER PATTERN: Our Father God, we believe that we have touched only the hem of your garment. Help us to wait for you until the full vision comes. Amen.